PROMOTING ELEMENTARY SCHOOL PHYSICAL ACTIVITY

IDEAS FOR ENJOYABLE ACTIVE LEARNING

Russell R. Pate

University of South Carolina

Ruth P. Saunders

University of South Carolina

HUMAN KINETICS

Library of Congress Cataloging-in-Publication Data

Names: Pate, Russell R., author. | Saunders, Ruth P., author.
Title: Promoting elementary school physical activity : ideas for enjoyable
active learning / Russell R. Pate, Ruth P. Saunders.
Description: Champaign, IL : Human Kinetics, 2024. | Includes
bibliographical references.
Identifiers: LCCN 2022041852 (print) | LCCN 2022041853 (ebook) | ISBN
9781718214743 (paperback) | ISBN 9781718214750 (epub) | ISBN
9781718214767 (pdf)
Subjects: LCSH: Physical education and training--Study and teaching
(Elementary)--United States. | Physical education for children--United
States. | Physical fitness for children--United States. | Active
learning--United States.
Classification: LCC GV365 .P37 2024 (print) | LCC GV365 (ebook) | DDC
372.86/0440973--dc23/eng/20221025
LC record available at https://lccn.loc.gov/2022041852
LC ebook record available at https://lccn.loc.gov/2022041853

ISBN: 978-1-7182-1474-3 (print)

Copyright © 2024 by Human Kinetics, Inc.

The web addresses cited in this text were current as of September 2023, unless otherwise noted.

Acquisitions Editor: Scott Wikgren; **Managing Editor:** Amanda S. Ewing; **Copyeditor:** Joanna Hatzopoulos Portman; **Proofreader:** Leigh Keylock; **Permissions Manager:** Laurel Mitchell; **Graphic Designer:** Denise Lowry; **Cover Designer:** Keri Evans; **Cover Design Specialist:** Susan Rothermel Allen; **Photograph (cover):** SeventyFour/iStock/Getty Images; **Photo Asset Manager:** Laura Fitch; **Photo Production Manager:** Jason Allen; **Senior Art Manager:** Kelly Hendren; **Illustrations:** © Human Kinetics, unless otherwise noted; **Printer:** Color House Graphics, Inc.

Printed in the United States of America   10 9 8 7 6 5 4 3 2 1

The paper in this book is certified under a sustainable forestry program.

Human Kinetics
1607 N. Market Street
Champaign, IL 61820
USA

United States and International
Website: **US.HumanKinetics.com**
Email: info@hkusa.com
Phone: 1-800-747-4457

Canada
Website: **Canada.HumanKinetics.com**
Email: info@hkcanada.com

CONTENTS

Part I
Classroom Physical Activity   1

Chapter 1   Classroom Physical Activity Breaks   3

Learn more about classroom physical activity breaks, which are brief times for physical activity in the classroom between periods of instruction and before, during, or after transitions throughout the day.

Chapter 2   Physically Active Instruction   19

Learn more about physically active instruction, where the teacher incorporates bouts of physical activity into academic instruction.

Chapter 3   Recess   41

Learn more about recess, which is a regularly scheduled period within the school day for physical activity and play.

Chapter 4   The Physically Active Classroom   59

Learn more about physically active classrooms, which combine nontraditional arrangements of the space and student-centered learning to reduce barriers to physical activity in the classroom.

Part II
Physical Education   73

Chapter 5   Enhanced Physical Education   75

Learn more about enhanced physical education, which involves curricula and practice-based approaches that aim to increase the amount of time students engage in moderate to vigorous physical activity during physical education classes.

Chapter 6   Physical Education Beyond the Gymnasium   95

Learn more about physical education beyond the gymnasium, where the physical education teacher creates a positive, motivational climate that results in students wanting to be physically active, connects them to physical activity opportunities during out-of-school time, and communicates with families about physical activity.

Part III
The Physically Active School   105

Chapter 7   Physical Activity Before and After School   107

Learn more about physical activity programs that provide supervised opportunities for children to be physically active immediately before and after school.

Chapter 8   The Physically Active School Environment   115

Learn more about the four interacting parts of the physically active school environment: physical environment, social environment related to physical activity, physical activity policies, and physical activity practices.

Chapter 9   Comprehensive School Physical Activity Program   127

Learn more about the five components of a comprehensive school physical activity program: physical education, physical activity during school, physical activity before and after school, staff involvement, and family and community engagement.

ACKNOWLEDGMENTS

Promoting Elementary School Physical Activity: Ideas for Enjoyable Active Learning arose from nearly 30 years of Children's Physical Activity Research Group (CPARG) experience with studying and promoting child and adolescent physical activity. We are indebted to our CPARG colleagues; we give special thanks to Kerry Cordan, Sharon Ross, and Dale Murrie, who developed the precursor document that ultimately grew into this book. We thank Laura Wentzski for her careful review and thoughtful feedback on the first draft of the book from an elementary school teacher's perspective. We are grateful for the generosity of Ellen Essick of North Carolina Healthy Schools and Eloise Elliott of eLearning for Kids Inc. for sharing physical activity ideas from their websites. We also thank authors Terry Orlick (*Cooperative Games, Second Edition*, 2006), Dale N. Le Fevre (*Best New Games, Updated Edition*, 2012), and Heather Gardner (*Physical Literacy on the Move*, 2017) for sharing physical activity ideas from their books. We appreciate your commitment to promoting fun childhood physical activity and learning. Finally, on behalf of CPARG, we express our deep gratitude to the schools, teachers, and students who have worked with us over the years.

INTRODUCTION

Imagine something natural, safe, and simple that helps children grow, stay healthy, manage stress, behave better in the classroom, and learn more effectively. If such a benefit existed, wouldn't every teacher and parent want it for their children? In fact, it does exist—in the form of regular physical activity—and every teacher has the means to use it as a tool.

Promoting Elementary School Physical Activity: Ideas for Enjoyable Active Learning (referred to as *IDEAL* throughout this text) provides practical and accessible ideas for using physical activity in the school setting. These ideas are backed up by evidence supporting the benefits of physical activity in the classroom. *IDEAL* is a tool that physical education and classroom teachers can use to transform school into a fun environment for learning and growing.

Children need physical activity to

- support their growth and development,
- stay healthy and avoid excessive weight gain,
- become skillful movers,
- learn effectively, and
- manage their mood and behavior in the classroom (figure I.1).

Physical activity in childhood helps build lifelong healthy habits. Because higher levels of physical activity are linked to better physical health as well as social, emotional, cognitive, and academic outcomes in children, the U.S. Department of Health and Human Services (HHS) issued physical activity guidelines for school-aged children and adolescents (HHS, 2018b). These guidelines call for children to engage in at least 60 minutes of moderate to vigorous physical activity daily. Further, HHS recommends that children engage in muscle-strengthening and bone-loading physical activity at least three days a week. The HHS guidelines also urge adults who influence the behavior of children to "provide young people opportunities and encouragement to participate in physical activities that are appropriate for their age, that are enjoyable, and that offer variety" (p. 48).

The HHS guidelines make a compelling case for the importance of physical activity to the health and development of children and adolescents. Unfortunately, evidence indicates that most young people in the United States do not meet those guidelines. The U.S. Centers for Disease Control and Prevention (CDC) reported that fewer than one-quarter

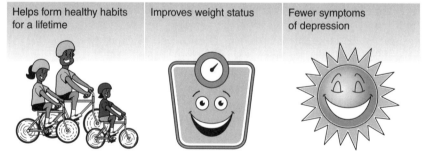

Figure I.1   Benefits of physical activity in children.

Information from Powell et al. (2018); HHS (2018a); HHS (2018b); CDC (2018); Lopes et al. (2021); Robinson et al. (2015); Hayes et al. (2019); Howie et al. (2020).

From R.R. Pate and R.P. Saunders, *Promoting Elementary School Physical Activity: Ideas for Enjoyable Active Learning* (Champaign, IL: Human Kinetics, 2024).

of 6- to 17-year-olds meet the 60-minute daily physical activity guideline (Merlo et al., 2020). Only about one-half of high school students engage in muscle-strengthening physical activity on three or more days a week. However, these figures are not surprising given that the rate of physical activity in the United States has declined with changes in lifestyle in recent decades. Motor vehicles have essentially replaced active forms of transport, and occupations have become increasingly sedentary. Even household chores such as cleaning, washing, and yard work no longer demand the level of physical activity that they once did. The use of electronic devices for recreation and diversion has replaced physically active pursuits with sedentary behaviors. Modern conveniences have markedly reduced—indeed almost eliminated—the outright demand for physical activity in daily life.

Reason for Optimism

The current status of physical activity in U.S. children is troubling, and the challenges associated with changing that status may seem daunting. However, much research has pointed to strategies that result in increasing physical activity in children. For example, kids who spend more time outside are more physically active than kids who don't spend much time outdoors. Kids are more physically active if their parents are physically active with them, if they have opportunities to participate in sports and physically active clubs and lessons, and if their home environment includes toys and implements to support physical activity (e.g., bicycles, balls, hoops).

Fortunately, research has shown that schools can provide their students with amounts of physical activity that make a real difference, resulting in many more kids meeting physical activity guidelines. Physical activity also enhances student attention, classroom behavior, and learning, which helps establish an enjoyable classroom environment in addition to promoting students' mental and physical health. Therefore, both classroom and physical education teachers play important roles in providing opportunities for students to move.

Rising to the Challenge

Teachers interact with students daily to provide instruction, build a positive learning environment, and serve as mentors and role models. With these demanding responsibilities, classroom teachers may feel that providing time for children to be active during the day is too much because they lack time, space, and equipment. *IDEAL* was developed as a way to solve this common problem. Most of the physical activity ideas in *IDEAL* are brief. In addition, their flexibility allows them to match existing curricula, classroom space, and resources as well as students'

FatCamera/E+/Getty

Children enjoy physical activity, which provides many physical, mental, social, and academic benefits.

needs and interests. *IDEAL* includes easy and creative ideas for activities that can be modified and expanded to help teachers provide a fun and engaging environment for learning.

No equipment is needed for most activities, and instructions are provided to make simple equipment from natural materials. For example, you can create a ball using tape over bunched-up newspapers. You can carry out most activities in small spaces or within your existing classroom setup. In short, as you oversee your classroom, you can use these ideas to make it a more active and fun place to learn; provide cognitive, social, and emotional benefits to students; and build classroom community with engaging activities. *IDEAL* also offers strategies and activities that encourage even more physical activity during physical education by making simple modifications to existing activities, games, transition times, and class practices (e.g., distributing and collecting equipment).

IDEAL provides simple, creative strategies and activity examples that other teachers have used successfully. *IDEAL* was designed to help classroom and physical education teachers move toward a goal of providing children with the physical activity they need to stay healthy and learn effectively. Classroom strategies and physical activity suggestions are based on proven ideas for promoting physical activity in children of all abilities and in all elementary grades. You will find this *IDEAL* guidebook to be ideal for your class!

Staying With the Challenge

IDEAL was designed with your busy schedule of competing demands in mind. It provides guidance, ideas, and options; you make the final choices and decisions in a way that works for you and your students. Each chapter provides tips for overcoming the challenges that are specific to that section. Increasing the physical activity options may feel awkward at first, and some initial activities may not go as planned. However, that discomfort is part of the process. Stay with it, and your students will benefit greatly. Over time, it will become the new routine.

All changes—even the positive ones—can be challenging. Change is also a process that requires time, trial, and error. Just like your students, teachers can learn from mistakes, and the key to success is persistence. Think about how it felt when you first learned a new skill, such as riding a bicycle or driving a car. Every single step was uncertain and required deliberation. Sitting in the driver's seat or on the bike was awkward; it may have even felt as though you didn't belong there. At the beginning, all the details were met with questions. ("What is the proper way to insert the key? What direction does it turn? How hard should it be turned?") However, after practice, you didn't have to think about it anymore; now you simply use the vehicle to get to where you need to go. This is how change operates. With persistence, early challenges dissolve quietly into habit.

Book Organization

This book is organized into three sections so that you can easily find and select the strategies and physical activity ideas that work for you. Part I, Classroom Physical Activity, offers ideas for integrating classroom physical activity breaks, incorporating physical activity into academic instruction, taking advantage of recess, and creating a physically active classroom.

Part II, Physical Education, is written specifically for the physical education teacher. It provides simple strategies for getting and keeping students moving throughout physical education class, connecting them to physical activity resources in the school and community, and facilitating lifelong physical activity.

Part III, The Physically Active School, presents more options for student physical activity, including offering before- and after-school programs and physically active transport to and from school. The chapters in part III also focus on the importance of the physical, policy, practice, and social environments for promoting school physical activity and the comprehensive school physical activity program as a tool to organize and coordinate the physical activity opportunities presented throughout *IDEAL*.

The physical activity opportunities and physical activity promoting environments presented throughout *IDEAL* include all children regardless of income, race, ethnicity, sex, gender identity, sexual identity, religion, physical or mental ability, appearance, or other characteristics. Providing equitable, socially just, and inclusive experiences for children necessarily involves learning about their family and community contexts prior to enacting school policies, programs, and practices (McMullen & Walton-Fisette, 2022). Therefore, the importance of family and community are emphasized throughout *IDEAL*.

Definitions Used Throughout the Book

Each chapter of this book provides definitions for key concepts within that chapter. The following definitions apply to all sections.

physical activity—Any bodily movement that increases heart rate, breathing, and sweating above resting levels. It includes structured exercise, playing sports, unorganized game play, active transport, and many other activities.

classroom physical activity—Any physical activity done in the classroom. It can take place at any time in the classroom, either integrated into instruction or outside of planned instruction. It is in addition to physical education and recess (CDC, 2018).

exercise—Physical activity that is structured and with the purpose of improving one or more components of physical fitness.

sedentary behavior—Lack of physical activity. It is characterized by no change from rest in heart rate, breathing, or sweating. Examples include lying down, sitting still, and standing still.

moderate to vigorous physical activity—Physical activity that is done with a moderate or higher (hard or very hard) effort. It causes noticeable increases in heart rate, breathing, and sweating. Examples include brisk walking, jogging, running, playing basketball, playing soccer, fast bicycling, and swimming.

transition time—The time between organized activity that is used to move between locations, change tasks, or gather materials. This time is an opportunity for more physical activity to be added to the school day.

Summary

IDEAL presents ideas, tips, suggestions, and examples you can use or adapt for your students. You choose how best to incorporate suggestions for physical activity opportunities into your classroom and school. *IDEAL* was created to make it easier for you to bring the fun of physical activity—along with its academic, social, and health benefits—to your students. The rest is up to you.

CLASSROOM PHYSICAL ACTIVITY

Part I is written for the elementary classroom teacher. This section of the book presents practical ideas that teachers can use to integrate physical activity into the classroom during the school day, ensure that students get time for recess, and shape the classroom as a physical activity–friendly place.

Chapter 1 (Classroom Physical Activity Breaks) and chapter 2 (Physically Active Instruction) describe the health, cognitive, and academic benefits of integrating physical activity breaks and physically active instruction (math, language arts, science, and social studies) into the school day. Short and simple physical activity tips, ideas, and examples—many of which are done deskside—are provided.

Chapter 3 (Recess) describes the benefits of play, recess, and enhanced recess for children, and it provides easy ideas and examples to use during recess. This chapter also addresses overcoming challenges from weather, air quality, and sun exposure, and it provides guidance on healthy hydration.

Chapter 4 (The Physically Active Classroom) describes the elementary classroom as a place that makes both academic learning and physical activity easy and natural. Nontraditional spaces, student-centered learning, and a positive, motivational climate contribute to less sitting, more moving, and more learning in class.

CHAPTER 1
CLASSROOM PHYSICAL ACTIVITY BREAKS

Quick Start

- *What?* Classroom physical activity breaks are brief times for students to be physically active in the classroom between periods of instruction and before, during, or after transitional times throughout the day. These short breaks do not involve integrating physical activity into instructional time.

- *Why?* Physical activity breaks improve attention and time on task (how much time elementary children spend actively involved in a task). They are also compatible with effective classroom management, and they contribute to children's daily physical activity.

- *Where?* Physical activity breaks can take place in any classroom, learning space, or other space in the school. Many physical activities can be done deskside.

- *Who?* All children in any classroom should participate. You can lead the activity break, show an active video to guide the activity, or get a student to demonstrate a physical activity or lead the class.

- *How long?* Physical activity breaks are usually brief (4-10 minutes). You can decide how long—or short—the breaks will be.

- *When?* Physical activity breaks can take place any time. They can occur at the beginning of the school day or class, during an academic class, or as a transition between different subjects. They are brief, so including multiple breaks in one day is easy. Physical activity breaks do not take the place of recess or physical education.

Easy Ideas
- Put on music and let children dance.
- Introduce short bursts of physical activity just before starting or ending class.
- Add more physical activity to transition times by allowing children to skip, hop, gallop, or march from place to place.
- Allow movements that can be performed vigorously at students' desks, such as the following (CDC, 2018):
  - Jumping jacks
  - Vertical jumps
  - Side-to-side jumps
  - Running in place
  - Squat jumps
  - High knees
  - Swimming strokes (front and back)
  - Arm circles (forward and backward)
  - Punches

Details

In addition to providing more details about benefits of classroom physical activity breaks, this section includes information you can share with administrators, other teachers and school staff, and parents.

Why Is This Important?

Physical activity breaks in elementary school classrooms have been well studied. Their benefits are documented through published scientific review articles and professional reviews of research evidence by groups such as the Physical Activity Guidelines Advisory Committee (HHS, 2018) and the Community Preventive Services Task Force (2021). Physical activity breaks

- add small but meaningful amounts of physical activity to the school day (Bassett et al., 2013),
- result in more student time on task during lessons following the breaks, and
- improve student attention in the time following breaks (HHS, 2018; Hillman et al., 2019; Community Preventive Services Task Force, 2021; Masini et al., 2020; Salmon et al., 2020).

Physically active breaks are also compatible and self-reinforcing with effective classroom management (Moon et al., 2020).

How Much Is Enough?

The most consistent benefits come with at least 10 minutes of moderate to vigorous physical activity (Sember et al., 2020); to achieve the same benefits, shorter time frames require vigorous physical activity (Daly-Smith et al., 2018). Therefore, children need to be very active during these brief breaks.

What Principals, Teachers, and Parents Need to Know

Figure 1.1 summarizes the key benefits of classroom physical activity breaks. Share this information with administrators, teachers, staff, parents, and others.

Using Physical Activity Breaks in Your Classroom

Information in the following sections is from CDC Classroom Physical Activity Ideas and Tips (cdc. gov); CDC, 2018; North Carolina Healthy Schools; Michael et al., 2019; and Van den Berg et al., 2017.

Quick Tips provides suggestions to get you off to a fast start. Ideas to Try When You Are Ready are great suggestions that are more involved to carry out. Things to Consider provides practical pointers for using physical activity breaks in your classroom. If you want more movement ideas for physically active breaks *now*, go to the section Physical Activity Ideas for Active Breaks.

Quick Tips

- Schedule physical activity breaks and then integrate them into your daily classroom routine.
- Choose physical activities that will get and keep children moving and breathing hard (moderate to vigorous physical activity).
- Demonstrate the movements to your class at the beginning of each activity.
- Model healthy behavior; encourage your students to move by participating in physical activity with them. If instruction is virtual, encourage parents, caregivers, siblings, guardians, and other household members to join in when possible.
- Verbally—and enthusiastically—encourage the students to join in and move.
- Mix it up. All of the ideas are flexible and can be customized. Change the prompts, rotate the movements or exercises, and vary the length of the activity. Make it work for you and your students.

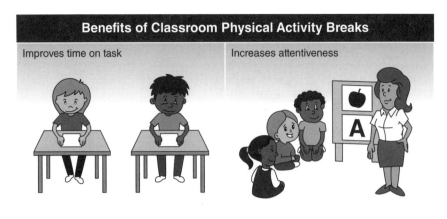

Figure 1.1 Benefits of classroom physical activity breaks.

Information from HHS (2018) and Community Preventive Services Task Force (2021).

From R.R. Pate and R.P. Saunders, *Promoting Elementary School Physical Activity: Ideas for Enjoyable Active Learning* (Champaign, IL: Human Kinetics, 2024).

- Play music. Use a song or tune to signify a movement break.
- Be mindful of different abilities and provide various movement choices or make modifications (e.g., arm circles instead of jumping jacks, doing activities from a seated position instead of a standing position). Let students know that it is all right to engage in a different physical activity; the idea is to take a break and move.
- When doing virtual learning, keep in mind where students are physically located (e.g., in a community center, at home in a crowded space) and how that place might affect their ability to participate in physical activity.

Ideas to Try When You Are Ready

- Communicate with parents and caregivers about the importance of physical activity. Let them know about the types of classroom activities students are doing and the benefits of these activities so that they know what to expect, understand the purpose, and can support and reinforce participation.
- Ask students to share their physical activity ideas. Give them the opportunity to choose the physical activity idea or to lead the activities.
- Partner with a physical education teacher, other interested staff, parents, or other volunteers for more physical activity break ideas.

Things to Consider

IDEAL is designed to minimize your preparation ahead of time; however, thinking through how this will work in your classroom does have benefits. The simple ideas presented next will help you get ready. Remember that all the ideas are flexible and can be customized. Change the prompts, rotate the movements or exercises, and vary the length of the activity. Make it work for you and your students.

Be Prepared

Start small with a physical activity that fits your comfort level and that you believe your students will like. Select a specific physical activity idea from *IDEAL* or another resource ahead of time and have a plan for when you will use the activity breaks. Gather any needed materials, equipment, technology, or other resources ahead of time. (Remember that most *IDEAL* physical activity breaks do not require materials or equipment.) Think about classroom space and how you can work with it or how you can modify your existing space (e.g., by moving furniture) to make it more activity friendly. Note that many physical activities can be done while students are standing beside their desks.

Keep It Fun

Involve all students, encourage them to be physically active, and join in the fun. Make physical activity a game. Add music that your students like. Look for opportunities during the day for brief bouts of physical activity. As you get comfortable and students learn the routine, add more breaks and different physical activities. Consider creating a class goal for number of minutes or activities; chart or graph it as a class activity. Refrain from withholding or using physical activity as punishment.

Manage Classroom Behavior

Establish rules, routines, and standards for behavior. The physically active break should have a clear and consistent beginning and end. Some level of noise during physical activities is expected, but you can work with your students on the appropriate levels for your class and school. Use a consistent transition back to academics, which you can signal in one of the following ways:

- Ring a bell.
- End with a silent activity.
- Play calming music.
- Initiate a clapping sequence; students respond by clapping the same sequence.
- Dim the lights briefly.
- End with a breathing exercise (e.g., breathe in for 3 seconds, hold for 3 seconds, breathe out for 3 seconds; take 5 deep breaths with the hands on the belly).
- End with some brief stretching, such as the following:
  - Gently drop the head toward the right shoulder and then toward the left shoulder.
  - Do shoulder shrugs or shoulder rolls.
  - Reach the arms toward the thighs, shins, or toes (bending knees as needed); reach the left arm to the right foot; reach the right arm to the left foot; and bend the torso over the thighs while holding opposite elbows (can sway hips).
  - Reach the arms up and wiggle the fingers, wiggle the toes, and rotate both wrists in each direction.

Overcome Challenges

Common challenges that classroom teachers report for carrying out these breaks are lack of time, lack of space, lack of resources such as equipment, lack of student involvement, and concerns about disruption. Conversely, facilitators are the perception that physical activity is valuable and using

skynesher/E+/Getty Images

Students can engage in many physical activity opportunities while standing beside their desks.

an approach that is feasible in the classroom—one that is quick, simple, and requires minimal or no equipment. The approach of *IDEAL* is based on these facilitating factors.

Many teachers believe that because of testing and other school pressures, it is not possible to set aside time for physical activity. If you are one of these teachers, reframe your thinking. Instead of trying to set aside separate time for physical activity, think about integrating brief bouts of simple, deskside exercises into your routine. You can choose the timing and select activities that require little or no preparation.

Notice who is participating and who is not with respect to factors such as race, gender, first language, physical or learning ability, and where students are seated. Explore reasons why some students may not be engaged and find opportunities to actively include these students. For example, some students may not know seemingly common terms for movements or games (e.g., jumping jacks) and therefore might not participate or feel included.

To manage potential chaos and disruption, delineate boundaries around physically active breaks. Each brief break has a clear beginning and end, which can come with a change in activity (e.g., a focus on stretching or breathing) or another signal (see the list in Manage Classroom Behavior).

Involve Others

In keeping with your schools' practices and policies, inform your principal, curriculum coordinator, school health staff, other teachers (including the physical education teacher), and parents about using physical activity breaks in your classroom. You can also approach interested teachers and staff, physical education teachers, and interested parents for ideas and support.

Physical Activity Ideas for Active Breaks

Specific ideas for physical activity breaks are presented in two sections: activities that can be done standing beside the desk and those that require a little more open space in the classroom (or elsewhere). These activities have been selected because they are simple and can be carried out briefly (4-10 minutes). The duration of each activity is flexible; you can adjust it based on the time you have. Table 1.1 provides an overview of the activities in this section.

Table 1.1   Sample Activities for Classroom Physical Activity Breaks

Name	Grades	Location
Morning Routine	K-5	Deskside
Up, Down, Stop, Go (Opposites, Antonyms)	1-5	Deskside
Four Walls	1-5	Deskside
Crazy Eights	1-5	Deskside
One Behind	1-5	Deskside
Movement Dice	1-5	Deskside
Red Light, Green Light	1-5	Deskside
The 12 Days of Fitness	3-5	Deskside
Freeze Dance Party	1-5	Open classroom or other space
Five-Minute Dance Party	1-5	Open classroom or other space
Moving 5-4-3-2-1	1-5	Open classroom or other space
Hit the Deck	2-5	Open classroom or other space

MORNING ROUTINE

Type: Classroom break (deskside)
Target grades: K-5
Equipment: None
Description: Have students begin the day with a series of simple physical activities lasting 30 seconds or more. Here are some examples:

- Jumping jacks
- Knee lifts
- Flapping arms like a bird
- Hopping
- Scissors (feet apart, then cross one foot in front; feet apart, then cross it in back; omit for K-1)

Follow each physical activity with a basic stretching movement. Here are some examples:

- Reaching for the sky
- Runner's stretch
- Butterfly stretch (sitting with soles of feet together)
- Knee to chest (standing, sitting, or lying)
- Ankle rotations (standing, sitting, or lying)

Hold stretches for 10 to 30 seconds. Repeat a different simple physical activity followed by a new basic stretch as many times as desired.

Courtesy of North Carolina Healthy Schools.

UP, DOWN, STOP, GO (OPPOSITES, ANTONYMS)

Type: Classroom break (deskside)
Target grades: 1-5
Equipment: None
Description: Call out the commands "Up," "Down," "Stop," or "Go" one at a time. Practice a few rounds before starting to model the physical activities as you call them out.

- Up: Students squat down.
- Down: Students jump or stretch up as high as possible.

- Stop: Students do a specific movement in the same spot (e.g., running, hopping in place).
- Go: Students freeze.

Variations:

- Ask a student to be the caller of the commands.
- Add other commands (e.g., "Fast," where students move slowly, or "Forward," where students face backward).

Adapted from "Springboard to Activate Schools - Classroom Physical Activity Ideas and Tips," Center for Disease Control and Prevention, accessed October 26, 2022, www.cdc.gov/healthyschools/physicalactivity/pdf/classroom_pa_ideas_and_tips_final_201008.pdf.

FOUR WALLS

Type: Classroom break (deskside)

Target grades: 1-5

Equipment: None

Description: Choose four different movements. Facing one wall of a room, prompt students to do a movement for 30 seconds. Ask them to face another wall, then prompt another movement. Repeat until all four walls are covered; it takes about two minutes. Repeat the four-wall sequence as time allows. Here are some movement examples:

- Jumping jacks
- Vertical jumps
- Arm circles (forward and backward)
- Side-to-side jumps
- Running in place
- Squat jumps
- Toe touches

Variations: For one of the walls, let students choose their own movement, or prompt them to act out their favorite physical activity.

Adapted from "Springboard to Activate Schools - Classroom Physical Activity Ideas and Tips," Center for Disease Control and Prevention, accessed October 26, 2022, www.cdc.gov/healthyschools/physicalactivity/pdf/classroom_pa_ideas_and_tips_final_201008.pdf.

CRAZY EIGHTS

Type: Classroom break (deskside)

Target grades: 1-5

Equipment: None

Description: Choose four different exercises and ask students to do each exercise eight times. Examples of exercises include the following:

- Jumping jacks
- Silly shakes (shake as silly as they can)
- High knees
- Punches
- Lunges

Tip: Include both upper- and lower-body movements.

Variations: Vary the exercises by adding the students' favorite exercises.

Adapted from "Springboard to Activate Schools - Classroom Physical Activity Ideas and Tips," Center for Disease Control and Prevention, accessed October 26, 2022, www.cdc.gov/healthyschools/physicalactivity/pdf/classroom_pa_ideas_and_tips_final_201008.pdf.

ONE BEHIND

Type: Classroom break (deskside)

Target grades: 1-5

Equipment: None

Description:

- The leader assembles the group so that the group can see the leader. Then the leader makes a simple movement and repeats it, such as lifting and lowering the right arm. For this first movement, the group is instructed to do nothing.
- After about five arm lifts, the leader makes a new movement, such as stretching the left hand to touch the toes. Now the group starts to do the first movement the leader made (lifting the right arm).
- When the leader changes the movement again (e.g., walking in place), the group does the movement the leader just finished (reaching for the toes with the left hand). This pattern continues; the group does the movement the leader has just done (the *one behind*).

Tips:

- Select movements that everyone can do.
- Tell students not to worry if they cannot remember the last movement the leader did. Somebody else in the group will remember, and they are allowed to copy that person.

Adapted by permission from D.N. Le Fevre, *Best New Games,* Updated Edition (Champaign, IL: Human Kinetics, 2012).

MOVEMENT DICE

Type: Classroom break (deskside)

Target grades: 1-5

Equipment: One die

Description: On the board, write a movement for each number of a die (or have students select their favorite activities). Roll the die, and have students do the movement the number of times corresponding to the number rolled. For example, if you roll a 4, have students do four jumping jacks; if you roll a 3, have students do three toe touches. Examples of exercises for each number on the die include the following:

- 1: Squat
- 2: Jumps
- 3: Toe touches
- 4: Jumping jacks
- 5: High knees
- 6: Running in place (two foot-touches to the floor = 1 count)

Variations:

- Add another die or roll the same die twice to add, subtract, divide, or multiply the number of repetitions. For example, 2 is rolled for jumping and 4 is rolled on another die. Ask the class, "How many jumps are we going to do? What is 2 plus 4?"
- If you don't have dice, you can search online for a virtual die roller.

Adapted from "Springboard to Activate Schools - Classroom Physical Activity Ideas and Tips," Center for Disease Control and Prevention, accessed October 26, 2022, www.cdc.gov/healthyschools/physicalactivity/pdf/classroom_pa_ideas_and_tips_final_201008.pdf.

RED LIGHT, GREEN LIGHT

Type: Classroom break (deskside)

Target grades: 1-5

Equipment: None

Description: Choose an action for students to copy. Say the following to change the speed of the action:

- "Red light" = Freeze in place
- "Yellow light" = Slow down the action
- "Green light" = Repeat the action as fast as possible

Variations: Once students are familiar with the physical activity, ask them to take turns leading or coming up with the movements.

Adapted from "Springboard to Activate Schools - Classroom Physical Activity Ideas and Tips," Center for Disease Control and Prevention, accessed October 26, 2022, www.cdc.gov/healthyschools/physicalactivity/pdf/classroom_pa_ideas_and_tips_final_201008.pdf.

THE 12 DAYS OF FITNESS

Type: Classroom break (deskside)

Target grades: 3-5

Equipment: None

Description: Using the holiday tune "The 12 Days of Christmas," students act out the following fitness song. "On the first day of fitness, my trainer gave to me . . . "

- 12 jumping jacks
- 11 reaches for the sky
- 10 knee lifts
- 9 side stretches
- 8 jogs in place
- 7 jabs or punches
- 6 kicks to the front
- 5 hip circles
- 4 jumping ropes (imaginary rope)
- 3 muscle poses ("Show your muscles")

- 2 lunges
- 1 stork stand (balance on one foot)

Variations:

- Write the physical activities on a board to make them easier for children to follow and to sing along.
- For a shorter version of the activity, have students sing the activities straight through without the repetitions in the original song.

Courtesy of North Carolina Healthy Schools.

FREEZE DANCE PARTY

Type: Classroom break (open classroom or other space)

Target grades: 1-5

Equipment: Music and equipment for playing it

Description: Play music for students to dance to, then stop it; when the music stops, students freeze. Start and stop the music multiple times.

Tip: Mark off personal space using floor tape or cones so that students have properly distanced boundaries.

Adapted from "Springboard to Activate Schools - Classroom Physical Activity Ideas and Tips," Center for Disease Control and Prevention, accessed October 26, 2022, www.cdc.gov/healthyschools/physicalactivity/pdf/classroom_pa_ideas_and_tips_final_201008.pdf.

FIVE-MINUTE DANCE PARTY

Type: Classroom break (open classroom or other space)

Target grades: 1-5

Equipment: A playlist and equipment for playing music

Description: Create a five-minute playlist for a dance party. Get students to do a different movement every time you change songs.

Variations: Use digital content designed to promote classroom physical activity (e.g., search online for Hip Hop Public Health or GoNoodle). Let students choose the songs, a video, and the movements.

Adapted from "Springboard to Activate Schools - Classroom Physical Activity Ideas and Tips," Center for Disease Control and Prevention, accessed October 26, 2022, www.cdc.gov/healthyschools/physicalactivity/pdf/classroom_pa_ideas_and_tips_final_201008.pdf.

MOVING 5-4-3-2-1

Type: Classroom break (open classroom or other space)

Target grades: 1-5

Equipment: None

Description: Ask students to touch or do five, four, three, and two things sequentially, then end with one calming breath (5-4-3-2-1). For example, students run in place 5 times, lunge 4 times, do 3 jumps, reach for the sky 2 times, and do 1 calming breath. For the breath, coach students this way: "Inhale deeply and slowly through your nose, allowing your belly to expand; exhale through your mouth with your lips lightly together and jaws relaxed." When it is safe to do so, incorporate variations of the physical activity: touch 5 tables, touch 4 walls, touch 3 chairs, do 2 high fives, take 1 calming breath; or, find 5 pencils, 4 red objects, 3 things made out of paper, 2 shiny objects, 1 thing you love; and so on.

Adapted from "Springboard to Activate Schools - Classroom Physical Activity Ideas and Tips," Center for Disease Control and Prevention, accessed October 26, 2022, www.cdc.gov/healthyschools/physicalactivity/pdf/classroom_pa_ideas_and_tips_final_201008.pdf.

HIT THE DECK

Type: Classroom break (open classroom or other space)

Target grades: 2-5

Equipment: A deck of cards

Description: Place a deck of cards in front of the class. Have one student select a card; students will do the corresponding physical activity for each suit. On a board, write the corresponding physical activities for each suit as follows:

- Heart: Touch elbow to knee or do crunches for 20 seconds.
- Diamond: Jog in place or march in place for 20 seconds.
- Club: Do modified push-ups or cabbage patch for 20 seconds.
- Spade: Do jumping jacks or scissors for 20 seconds.

Provide other students the opportunity to pick a card from the deck and repeat the activity.

Variations:

- To take this activity outside, write physical activities on chart paper.

- To save time, choose three or four cards of each suit instead of using the entire deck.
- Use this physical activity when you have a substitute teacher; it is easy for a substitute teacher to follow.

Courtesy of North Carolina Healthy Schools.

Summary

Classroom physical activity breaks provide 4- to 10-minute segments of time for students to participate in fun physical activity in the classroom between periods of instruction as well as before, during, or after transitional times throughout the day. Children can perform many activities while standing beside their desks. Physical activity breaks have been shown to improve attention and the length of time elementary children spend actively involved in a task (time on task). Physical activity breaks do not take the place of recess or physical education.

CHAPTER 2
PHYSICALLY ACTIVE INSTRUCTION

Quick Start

- *What?* In physically active instruction, the teacher incorporates bouts of physical activity into academic instruction. The physical activity is part of the lesson and does not stop instruction time.

- *Why?* Integrating bouts of physical activity into instruction has been shown to improve cognition, including attention, memory, general and verbal knowledge, processing speed, and executive control following exercise. Regular physical activity benefits the brain, cognition, and academic outcomes including academic achievement tests in preadolescent children.

- *Where?* Physically active instruction is done in the classroom or other instructional space, indoors or outdoors. Many activities can take place beside the students' desks or in open space in the classroom.

- *Who?* All students in the classroom should participate in physically active instruction. It is most frequently led by the classroom teacher.

- *How long?* The activities in physically active instruction range from 11 to 30 minutes in duration. They can be used one or more times per day, up to five days per week.

- *When?* Physically active instruction can be a part of any subject, including math, language arts, science, and social studies. As part of the instructional method, it can be used at any point during the lesson.

Quick Tips

- Physical activity may be integral to the learning task, such as counting the number of jumping jacks (or other exercises) performed as you do them.

- Physical activity may occur simultaneously with the learning task, such as using movements to show whether an answer is true or false.

Details

In addition to providing more details about benefits of physically active instruction, this section includes information you can share with administrators, other teachers and school staff, and parents.

Why Is This Important?

Strong evidence shows that bouts of moderate to vigorous physical activity improve children's cognition, including attention, general and verbal knowledge, processing speed, and executive control, during the period following the exercise (HHS, 2018). Evidence also indicates that both bouts and long-term moderate to vigorous physical activity benefit the brain, cognition, and academic outcomes including performance on academic achievement tests in preadolescent children (HHS, 2018; Hillman et al., 2019). Similarly, the Community Preventive Services Task Force found a large improvement in lesson-time educational outcomes and a small improvement in overall educational outcomes, including time on task and academic achievement (Community Preventive Services Task Force, 2021; Norris et al., 2020). Physically active instruction can also enhance classroom management (Moon et al., 2020).

How Much Is Enough?

The most consistent benefits come with at least 10 minutes of moderate to vigorous physical activity (Sember et al., 2020); to achieve the same benefits, shorter time frames require vigorous physical activity (Daly-Smith et al., 2018).

What Principals, Teachers, and Parents Need to Know

Figure 2.1 summarizes the key benefits of physically active instruction. Share this information with administrators, teachers, staff, parents, and others.

Using Physically Active Instruction in Your Classroom

Information in the following sections was adapted from CDC, 2018, CDC Springboard to Action, NC Healthy Schools, Michael et al., 2019, and Van den Berg et al., 2017.

Many of the principles for active breaks presented in chapter 1 apply to integrating physically active instruction. This chapter emphasizes those that are most relevant to active instruction.

Figure 2.1 Benefits of physically active instruction.

Information from HHS (2018) and Norris et al. (2020).

From R.R. Pate and R.P. Saunders, *Promoting Elementary School Physical Activity: Ideas for Enjoyable Active Learning* (Champaign, IL: Human Kinetics, 2024).

Quick Tips

- Include physical activity planning as part of your regular lesson planning.
- Choose activities that will get and keep students moving and breathing hard (moderate to vigorous physical activity).
- Demonstrate the movements to your class at the beginning of each activity.
- Participate in the activity with the students. If instruction is virtual, encourage parents, caregivers, siblings, guardians, and other household members to join in when possible.
- Verbally—and enthusiastically—encourage students to join in and move.
- Be mindful of different abilities and provide various choices or make modifications (e.g., arm circles instead of jumping jacks, doing activities from a seated position instead of a standing position). Let students know that it is all right to engage in a different physical activity; the idea is to take a break and move.
- When doing virtual learning, keep in mind where students are physically located (e.g., in a community center, at home in a crowded space) and how that place might affect their ability to participate in physical activity.

Things to Consider

The following simple suggestions will prepare you to carry out physically active instruction in your classroom so that you can minimize common challenges.

Be Prepared

Like all effective instruction, preparing for physically active instruction necessarily involves advance planning. *IDEAL* is designed to facilitate this process. As you follow your curriculum or other instructional guidelines, look for ways to integrate activity into the lessons at the beginning, middle, or end as a review. Using *IDEAL* and other resources, select activities by subject matter that fit with the lesson objectives, classroom space, and class time frame. Adapt the physical activity idea to work with your way of teaching and your instructional objectives.

Keep It Fun

Initially, select activities that you like and that you believe your students will like. Demonstrate the movements, join in the activity, and encourage everyone to participate. As you become more comfortable with activity while teaching, ask students what activities and movements they like and then come up with more ways to incorporate their favorites into lessons.

Manage Classroom Behavior

The ideas for classroom management covered in chapter 1 also apply to physically active instruction. In fact, the rules, routines, and standards for behavior that apply to active breaks can also apply to physically active instruction. Some level of noise during activities is expected, but you can work with your students on the appropriate levels for your class and for your school. Select a consistent signal for the transition from activity to academics (e.g., doing a silent activity, ringing a bell, dimming the lights briefly; see chapter 1).

Overcome Challenges

Many of the challenges covered for active breaks in chapter 1 also apply to active instruction. Particularly important for physically active instruction are lack of time, lack of space, and classroom management. The lack of time challenge comes from these sources:

- Sometimes the phrase *lack of time* actually means lower priority for physical activity. Constraints on the time available during the school day do exist; understanding the benefits of physically active instruction for academic outcomes is the most important way to overcome this barrier.

- Sometimes it refers to constraints on the time needed to plan or prepare for the lesson. The key to overcoming limits on planning and preparation time is to include physical activity planning as part of your regular lesson planning.

- Sometimes it refers to the time needed to carry out the active learning lessons. You can address this challenge by realizing that this physical activity time in the classroom is not for physical activity per se; it is part of the academic instruction, furthering academic goals and objectives. A simple and efficient way to start is with the active ideas that can be adapted to any subject (see table 2.1 for examples). *IDEAL* and other resources provide many time-saving physical activity ideas that can be incorporated into instruction; most of these activities can be done in the classroom.

The activities for physically active instruction in *IDEAL* have been selected to minimize the use of exercise equipment. However, equipment is sometimes needed. Consider making your own out of natural materials, such as creating balls using tape over crumpled newspapers. In several of the activities, learning materials are needed. Supporting materials are frequently used in instruction that does not involve physical activity, and you may have these or similar materials already available in your

Allen J. Schaben/Los Angeles Times via Getty Images

Physical activity can become an effective part of instruction in all subjects.

classroom. In most cases, the learning props use common educational supplies that need to be created only once.

Involve Others

As noted in chapter 1, it is important to communicate with parents and caregivers about the benefits of physical activity. Let them know about the types of classroom activities students are doing and why so that they know what to expect, understand the purpose, and can support and reinforce participation.

Partner with a physical education teacher to get more physical activity ideas and to involve that teacher in active academic instruction.

Physical Activity Ideas for Physically Active Instruction

Sample activities for physically active instruction in math, language arts, science, and social studies are summarized in table 2.1 and presented on the following pages. Several of the activities can be adapted to any subject, as indicated in the table. The best location for each activity is also indicated; some are done standing deskside, some are done in open space in the classroom, and a few require open space such as in a gym or outdoors.

Table 2.1   Sample Activities for Physically Active Instruction

Name	Subject	Grade(s)	Location
Scavenger Hunt	All subjects	1-5	Virtual
Rock, Paper, Scissors, Jump	All subjects	1-5	Deskside
Vote With Your Feet	All subjects	1-5	Open space in classroom
True, False	All subjects	1-5	Deskside
Language Lights	Can be adapted to all subjects	1-2	Deskside
Memory Match	Can be adapted to all subjects	4-5	Open space in classroom
Physical Activity Jeopardy	Math	1-5	Open space in classroom
Active Math Station Rotation	Math	2-3	Open space in classroom
Factor It In	Math	4-5	Open space in classroom
How Many Sounds in the Word?	Language arts	1	Deskside
Movement Spelling	Language arts	K-1	Open space in classroom
Space Jam	Language arts	K-3	Deskside
Stop and Scribble	Language arts	2-5	Deskside
Action Letters	Language arts	4-5	Deskside
Water Cycle Song	Science	1-2	Deskside
Earth, Air, Fire, Water	Science	1-2	Open space in classroom
Herbivore, Carnivore, Omnivore	Science	3-4	Open space in classroom (tag game)
Funny Bones	Science	5	Open space in classroom

(continued)

Table 2.1 *(continued)*

Name	Subject	Grade(s)	Location
Germs and Doctors	Social studies	K-5	Gym or outdoor space
California Dreamin'	Social studies	4-5	Open space in classroom
Presidential Race	Social studies	4-5	Gym

SCAVENGER HUNT

Activity type: Physically active instruction—all subjects

Target grades: 1-5

Equipment: List of items for the scavenger hunt

Description: This activity is done virtually. Give students a list of items to retrieve from their home and a time limit to retrieve them so that they move as quickly as possible (e.g., 15 items in 5 minutes). Examples include something red, something you wear on your head, and something that brings you joy. After the allotted time is up, go down the list and ask students to show what they found.

Variations:

- Tie in a few items for the next part of your lesson (e.g., for math, something that measures volume; for geography, an object that tells a story about a place; for literature, a book by a favorite author).
- This activity can be done in person if it is conducted outdoors.

Adapted from "Springboard to Activate Schools - Classroom Physical Activity Ideas and Tips," Center for Disease Control and Prevention, accessed October 26, 2022, www.cdc.gov/healthyschools/physicalactivity/pdf/classroom_pa_ideas_and_tips_final_201008.pdf.

ROCK, PAPER, SCISSORS, JUMP

Activity type: Physically active instruction—all subjects

Target grades: 1-5

Equipment: Multiple-choice questions in any subject

Description: Ask students multiple-choice questions and have them respond by jumping into the correct position. Students jump three times; on the fourth jump, they land in the position that corresponds to the correct answer choice:

- Choice A: Feet together
- Choice B: Feet apart in a straddle position
- Choice C: One foot in front of the other

Variations: Different activities can be used to indicate the correct answer.

Adapted from "Springboard to Activate Schools - Classroom Physical Activity Ideas and Tips," Center for Disease Control and Prevention, accessed October 26, 2022, www.cdc.gov/healthyschools/physicalactivity/pdf/classroom_pa_ideas_and_tips_final_201008.pdf.

VOTE WITH YOUR FEET

Activity type: Physically active instruction—all subjects

Target grades: 1-5

Equipment: Signs with the words *yes, no, true, false, agree*, and *disagree*

Description: Post around the classroom signs with the words *yes, no, true, false, agree*, and *disagree*. Depending on the day's lesson, ask students to answer questions by going to stand by the sign that best reflects their answer. If applicable, ask students to elaborate on their answers. If the classroom has ample space, ask students to actively move (e.g., hop, skip, lunge step) to their answer choice.

Variations: If the class is virtual, instead of signs around the classroom, use movement to indicate the response. For example, students do arm circles if they choose A; stretch overhead if they choose B; give themselves a big hug if they choose C.

Adapted from "Springboard to Activate Schools - Classroom Physical Activity Ideas and Tips," Center for Disease Control and Prevention, accessed October 26, 2022, www.cdc.gov/healthyschools/physicalactivity/pdf/classroom_pa_ideas_and_tips_final_201008.pdf.

TRUE, FALSE

Activity type: Physically active instruction—all subjects

Target grades: 1-5

Equipment: True and false statements to read to students

Description: Read each statement. Have students answer if statements are true or false by jumping in place for 10 seconds for "true"

and sitting back in a squat for 10 seconds for "false." This activity is good for reviewing and checking understanding of content.

Adapted from "Springboard to Activate Schools - Classroom Physical Activity Ideas and Tips," Center for Disease Control and Prevention, accessed October 26, 2022, www.cdc.gov/healthyschools/physicalactivity/pdf/classroom_pa_ideas_and_tips_final_201008.pdf.

LANGUAGE LIGHTS

Activity type: Physically active instruction—all subjects

Target grades: 1-2

Equipment: None

Description: Assign different movements to different types of letters or words and tell the students what they are. Here are examples of types of letters or words and movement types for a language lesson:

- Consonants: 5 jumping jacks
- Vowels: 5 toe touches
- Nouns: 5 reaches for the sky
- Verbs: 5 push-ups
- Adjectives: 5 squats

Call out a stoplight color, and have students move as the color dictates, such as the following:

- Red light: Students stop their movement.
- Yellow light: Students jog in place.
- Green light: Students pause for a second then you say one of the letters or words from the lesson. For example, if you say "b," *b* is a consonant, so the students must do 5 jumping jacks. If you say "u," *u* is a vowel, so the students must do 5 toe touches.
- Pit stop: Students stop and complete a stretch, holding it for eight seconds.

Variations: This lesson can be adapted for use in other subjects.

- Math: Assign numbers instead of word types, and have the students move based on whether the number is odd or even; is a whole, decimal, or fraction; is expressed in tens, hundreds, or thousands; is a square root or not; or is divisible by a particular number.

- Science: Instead of word types, assign animals, plants, simple machines, weather, or types of rock.
- Geography: Assign movement types to directions (north, east, south, west). Call out a state or country, and have the students move based on where the state or country is compared to their current location.

Courtesy of ActiveAcademics.org

MEMORY MATCH

Activity type: Physically active instruction—all subjects

Target grades: 4-5

Equipment: Cards or paper plates

Description: Write rhyming words, homonyms, or other matching words on pairs of paper plates or cards (one word on each plate or card). Scatter half of the paper plates or cards turned upside down around one side of the classroom playing space; scatter the matching paper plates or cards on the other side of the space.

Group students into pairs. Have each pair start at a different spot in the room and, using a specific locomotor pattern (e.g., hopping on one foot, skipping, twirling), move to one side of the space to pick a paper plate or card. Then have the students move, using the same locomotor pattern, to the other side of the space to find their matching word. Have them turn over a card. If they find a match, they bring both cards back to where they started; if the card doesn't match, they place it back on the floor upside down for the other teams to find and turn over another card until they find their match. Partners must stay together and can only turn over one card at a time.

Variations:

- Mathematics: Write equations on the paper plates or cards, and have the students match them with the correct solution.
- Social studies: Tape pictures and their matching words or dates (e.g., countries, cultures, historic figures, historic events) to the paper plates or cards, and have the students match the pictures to the words.

Courtesy of ActiveAcademics.org

PHYSICAL ACTIVITY JEOPARDY

Activity type: Physically active instruction—math

Target grades: 1-5

Equipment: 5 to 10 prepared cards or sheets of paper

Description: On one side of a card or piece of paper, write a physical activity movement; on the other side, write a number (e.g., 10, 15, 20, 25). Tape 5 to 10 cards or sheets of paper on a wall in the classroom with the activity side facing out. Call on a student to pick one of the cards. Have the class perform the physical activity on the card for the number of repetitions written while counting out loud. Here are some movement ideas:

- Boxing jabs
- Jumps
- Push-ups
- Triceps dips using chairs
- Arm circles
- Jumping jacks
- Elbow-to-opposite-knee touches (while standing)

Variations:

- If the class is virtual, search for a free online platform (e.g., Factile) to create a similar board.
- Provide alternative activities for different ability levels.

Adapted from "Springboard to Activate Schools - Classroom Physical Activity Ideas and Tips," Center for Disease Control and Prevention, accessed October 26, 2022, www.cdc.gov/healthyschools/physicalactivity/pdf/classroom_pa_ideas_and_tips_final_201008.pdf.

ACTIVE MATH STATION ROTATION

Activity type: Physically active instruction—math

Target grades: 2-3

Equipment: Grade-appropriate flash cards, construction paper, paper and pencils

Description: Set up four or more stations around your classroom. At each station, have a sign (on the construction paper) indicating what type of locomotor movement students should use to travel to the next station after they complete the math problems. Examples of locomotor movements include hopping, skipping, walking, and jogging. At each station, include a minimum of three flash cards with grade-appropriate math problems and a supply of paper and pencils.

Divide students into four or more groups, and number them 1 to 4 (or more if you have more stations). Distribute a sheet of paper to each student for recording answers to math problems from the flash cards. On the signal to begin, have students travel using any locomotor movement they choose to their first station. There, they will pick up a pencil, work the math problems on the flash cards, and write their answers on their paper. On the signal to change, they will perform the locomotor movement indicated on the movement sign at their station and travel to the next station. For safety, students should not carry the pencils from one station to the next.

Courtesy of ActiveAcademics.org

FACTOR IT IN

Activity type: Physically active instruction—math

Target grades: 4-5

Equipment: Four pieces of scrap paper labeled with numbers 2, 3, 4, and 5

Description: Display the list of movements from which students can select on a large sheet of paper or on a board. Examples include jumping, skipping, walking, hopping, and marching. Label each corner of the room with one of the pieces of scrap paper. Divide students into four groups and send each group to a corner of the room. Call out a number that is a multiple of 2, 3, 4, or 5. Students who are in a corner that is a factor of that number will select a movement to move to another corner. For example, if you call out "6," students in corners labeled 2 and 3 will move to another corner.

Variations: Have students move to a corner labeled with a factor of the number called. If a prime number is called, have students move to the center of the room.

Courtesy of North Carolina Healthy Schools.

HOW MANY SOUNDS IN THE WORD?

Activity type: Physically active instruction—language arts

Target grades: 1

Equipment: Music (optional)

Description: Guide the entire class through identifying the sounds in a word. Ask the students how many sounds are in a word by giving them options combined with a corresponding physical activity. For example, if students think the correct answer is 4, they run in place; if they think it's 3, they do jumping jacks. This approach allows you to quickly assess how many students comprehend the concept while using whole-group responses. This activity is effective to use while students are working in their practice books, and it can be combined with bursts of dancing to music.

Courtesy of ActiveAcademics.org

MOVEMENT SPELLING

Activity type: Physically active instruction—language arts

Target grades: K-1

Equipment: Index cards

Description: Create letter cards using the index cards. You could use the spelling word list for the week or create your own list, such as a list of animals (e.g., bear, snake, horse, hen, frog). Write one of each letter onto the index cards; for example, for *bear*, use separate index cards for *B*, *E*, *A*, and *R*. If you have more students playing than letters in each word, create duplicate letters until you equal the number of children playing. Repeat for each of the words, creating a separate collection of letter cards.

Hand out the first set of letter cards. When each student gets a letter, announce the mystery word (in this case, *bears*). Ask the class, "What is the first letter in *bears*?" Everyone with *B* cards should move like a bear to the front of the room. Ask, "What is the next letter in *bears*?" Everyone with *E* cards should move like a bear to the front of the room. Continue until the word is spelled. Have the students move like bears for a while, then hand out a new set of cards.

If you are doing a spelling list, you can set the movement for each word. For example, the word is *sunshine*. Hand out the cards, and have the children move to the front of the room with their letter cards by jumping forward each time. Change the movement for the next word.

Variations:

- To make the activity more challenging, hand out the set of cards for one word and give extra children all the same letter (that is not in the spelling word). For example, if you have 20 students in the class and the word is *sunshine*, hand out each letter in the word (8 cards) plus 12 cards, all with a *D* on them. Now students have to move around the room with whatever locomotor action you call out to unscramble the spelling word. All the students with more than one matching letter should exclude themselves from being in the spelling word.

- To make the activity easier, write the spelling word on the board to provide a visual cue to match the letters on the board to the index card. For nonambulatory students, when the letter is called, have them try movement actions such as raising the right arm, waving the left hand, nodding the head, or hitting a switch.

- To encourage vigorous physical activity, try the game outdoors to practice running.

Courtesy of ActiveAcademics.org

SPACE JAM

Activity type: Physically active instruction—language arts

Target grades: K-3

Equipment: None

Description: Read the following story to the students. The students identify each verb (or use the term *action word*). Pause during reading so that the students can act out each verb in place for 15 to 20 seconds. Continue until the end of the story. Here's the story (with the recommended movements set in bold):

Hello, my name is Zippy, and I live on a space station. Today, I will lead you on a tour through space. First, we need to **put on our moon boots**. They will allow us to walk through space. The first stop is Mercury, the closest planet to the sun. Mercury is very hot, so—ouch—be careful and **step quickly so that your feet do not get burned**. Mercury also has many craters. On the count of 3, let's jump into a crater and see what we find. 1, 2, 3, **jump!**

Climb out of the crater so that we can **march to Venus**. Venus is the second planet from the sun. This planet has very strong winds and volcanoes. See if you can **walk through the wind without blowing over**.

A lot of the surface of Venus is covered with lava, and here comes some lava now. **Run**!

The next stop is Earth, the third planet from the sun. Seventy-one percent of Earth's surface is water, so **hop in and start swimming**. See if you can **do the front crawl and the backstroke**.

Our next stop is Mars. Mars is known as the red planet. The largest mountain in space, Olympic Mons, is located on Mars. See if you can **climb to the top**.

Jupiter is the fifth planet from the sun. It is made up of mostly gas, and you can see clouds when you look at this planet. **Find a cloud** and see if you can **float on it.**

Our next stop is Saturn, the sixth planet from the sun. It has a rocky core, and areas of ice are located throughout the planet. Rings of gases surround Saturn. Whoa, I see a huge piece of ice; **be careful, and slide across it. Hop on one of the rings** surrounding Saturn, and **spin around in circles**.

Uranus is our next stop. It has a small rocky core. Can everyone **tiptoe across Uranus watching out for the ice**?

Next, let's visit Neptune. Neptune has four rings and large storms with fast winds. It also has 13 moons. **Quick, duck!** Here comes a moon, **move to the left** so you do not get hit.

Pluto is our last stop. It is the smallest planet, and it is farthest from the sun. Because it is so far from the hot sun, Pluto is a cold planet. **Shiver, and rub your hands** together to stay warm.

This ends our tour of space. **Grab a partner and hop back to the space station**.

Courtesy of North Carolina Healthy Schools.

STOP AND SCRIBBLE

Activity type: Physically active instruction—language arts

Target grades: 2-5

Equipment: A piece of paper and pencil for every pair of students

Description: Group students into pairs and give each pair a piece of paper and a pencil. Call out a physical activity movement, such as jumping, twisting, jogging, jumping jacks, hopping, knee lifts, playing air guitar, or marching. Students will begin the movement and continue until you call out a spelling word. When students stop the movement, partners work together to try to spell the word correctly on their piece of paper. After 10 to 15 seconds, call out a new movement.

Continue until all spelling words are used. As students cool down, write the correct spelling on a board, and have students check their work.

Variation: Do this activity outside and use sidewalk chalk instead of paper and pencils.

Courtesy of North Carolina Healthy Schools.

ACTION LETTERS

Activity type: Physically active instruction—language arts

Target grades: 4-5

Equipment: None

Description: Prior to the activity, choose actions for certain letters of the alphabet. To keep this lesson highly active, choose the most common letters for the week's spelling or vocabulary words. Vowels always work well. Write them on the board. Here are examples:

A: High knees

D: Jumping jack

E: Front kick

L: Right punch

O: Reach for the sky

P: Scissors kick

R: Left punch

Have students stand next to their desks. Give the students a spelling or vocabulary word to spell out loud as a group. When they get to one of the action letters, they must say the letter and do the action. For example, ask the students to spell *hyperbole*. The group will stand still and say "H," say "Y," scissors kick while saying "P," front kick while saying "E," punch left while saying "R," stay still while saying "B," reach for the sky while saying "O," punch right while saying "L," and end with another front kick while saying "E." Have students start and end each word in spelling bee fashion (saying the word out loud together as a group before and after spelling the word).

Variations: Another way to play Action Letters is to substitute certain motions for vowels and consonants. For example, a hop on one foot could represent a vowel while an air punch could represent a consonant.

Courtesy of ActiveAcademics.org

WATER CYCLE SONG

Activity type: Physically active instruction—science

Target grades: 1-2

Equipment: None

Description: Use the water cycle song when teaching that water can be a solid, liquid, or gas. It reinforces vocabulary (*evaporation, condensation, precipitation, accumulation*) and reinforces that the water cycle is a repeating pattern. This song is to the tune of "Clementine."

"Evaporation": Push both arms up.

"Condensation": Push with both arms straight out to the sides.

"Precipitation on my head": Pretend to rain on head.

"Accumulation": Sweep arms in front.

"Water cycle": Arms rotate in circle in front.

"And it starts all over again": Turn around in a circle in place.

Courtesy of ActiveAcademics.org

EARTH, AIR, FIRE, WATER

Activity type: Physically active instruction—science

Target grades: 1-2

Equipment: Small- or medium-sized ball

Description: Have students form a circle; one student starts with the ball. The student tosses the ball to another student while at the same time calling out either of these words: *earth, air, water,* or *fire.*

- If the student calls out "Earth," other students march in place for 5 seconds until you say "Freeze." At that time, the player to whom the ball is tossed (the catcher) has to name something that lives on the earth (on land), such as a lion. The student has 10 seconds to answer and then tosses the ball to another person.
- If a student calls out "Air," the others act as if they are flying for 5 seconds, then the catcher must say something that lives in the air (e.g., a species of bird).
- If a student calls out "Water," the other students act as if they are swimming for 5 seconds, then the catcher must say something that lives in the water (e.g., a type of fish).
- If a student calls out "Fire," all the students freeze, and the catcher must keep silent.

Continue to play a few rounds until all students have had a turn to verbally respond with a living organism in the environment called out.

Variations: Students play the game standing by their desks; you call out the environment. After saying "Freeze," you then call on one or two students to identify a living organism before calling out another environment.

Courtesy of ActiveAcademics.org

HERBIVORE, CARNIVORE, OMNIVORE

Activity type: Physically active instruction—science

Target grades: 3-4

Equipment:

- Five slips of paper labeled *LIFE* for each student
- Colorful signs for each student to wear around the neck:
  - One labeled *HUMAN* (orange)
  - Two labeled *OMNIVORE* (yellow)
  - Four labeled *CARNIVORE* (blue)
  - Enough for remaining students labeled *HERBIVORE* (green)
- Green cones (or other green items, such as strips of green construction paper) representing grass for herbivores to "eat"

Description: Give each student their five *LIFE* strips and distribute a colorful sign to each student. Provide examples for each class of animals as follows:

- Herbivore: Rabbit, deer, elephant, giraffe, hippo, panda, bison, camel, cow, gorilla, horse, kangaroo, koala, reindeer, rhino, sheep, zebra
- Carnivore: Wolf, tiger, lion, fox, puma, hyena, otter, skunk, raccoon, seal, shark
- Omnivore: Pig, dog, bear, mouse, squirrel, hedgehog, chimpanzee

As students are given their colored sign, they choose an animal from the group color they were given (e.g., a giraffe as an herbivore).

Instruct students to play this game in a manner similar to tag. Students run or walk around and act like their chosen animal while trying to avoid being "eaten" (tagged).

- The human can tag herbivores, omnivores, and carnivores.
- Omnivores can tag carnivores or herbivores.
- Carnivores can tag only the herbivores.

- Herbivores can't tag anyone; instead, they try to survive by collecting as much "food" (green cones or strips of paper) as they can without being tagged.

If a student is tagged, that student gives up one "life" (slip of paper) to the person who tagged them (or to the teacher, depending on how you want to structure this activity). Once students are out of paper, they return to their seat, then perform a movement that the teacher designates (e.g., jumping jacks, walking in place, front kicks, right and left punches, reaches for the sky) or a favorite movement of their own choosing.

Courtesy of ActiveAcademics.org

FUNNY BONES

Activity type: Physically active instruction—science

Target grade: 5

Equipment: Instrumental recording of the song "Hokey Pokey"

Description: This activity is based on the song "Hokey Pokey." After teaching a lesson on the anatomical names of the bones of the body, tell the students to get in a circle formation. The students will sing and learn while they point to each body part identified and place that body part inside the circle. For example, "You put your tarsals in, you put your tarsals out, you put your tarsals in, and you shake them all about. You do the fun bone dance and turn yourself around. That's what it's all about!" Other examples of bones to identify include the fibula, sternum, radius, tibia, pelvis, carpals, humerus, patella, rib cage, ulna, cranium, and femur. At the end of the song, the whole class shakes their bodies, turns around in a circle, and sings, "You do the fun bone dance. You do the fun bone dance. That's what it's all about!"

Courtesy of ActiveAcademics.org

GERMS AND DOCTORS

Activity type: Physically active instruction—social studies

Target grades: K-5

Equipment: Ribbons or other indicators for germs and doctors

Description: For every 5 students, choose 1 to represent a germ; for every 10 students, choose 1 to represent a doctor. If your class has 20 students, you will have 4 germs and 2 doctors. When the game starts, the germs attempt to tag people, who then collapse on the ground (a crouch will suffice) and start calling out, "Doctor, Doctor!" One of the players designated as a doctor heals the sick person with a touch. That person then stands back up and attempts to avoid the germs. Of course, doctors can get sick, too, and they may need a doctor. If all the doctors get infected, no one can be cured any longer and the game ends. The game continues until everyone gets tired or all players are infected. This game goes quickly and can be repeated with students playing a different role.

Variations: If you have a small space, change locomotion to something slower than running.

Adapted by permission from D.N. Le Fevre, *Best New Games,* Updated Edition (Champaign, IL: Human Kinetics, 2012).

CALIFORNIA DREAMIN'

Activity type: Physically active instruction—social studies
Target grades: 4-5
Equipment: None
Description: Lead the class on a virtual tour of California. Students move at least 30 seconds for each of these actions:

- March across the Golden Gate Bridge.
- Surf in the Pacific Ocean.
- Climb up a redwood tree.
- Pretend you are an actor, and wave to all your fans.
- Flex your muscles like former Governor Arnold Schwarzenegger.
- Stomp on grapes to make juice.
- Pick oranges.
- In-line skate on the boardwalk.
- Ski down a mountain in the Sierra Nevadas.
- Climb Mount Whitney, the highest peak in the continental United States.
- Crawl through the Death Valley in the Mojave Desert.
- Hit a home run at Oracle Park.
- Shoot a foul shot at the Staples Center.

Variations: You can use a similar activity to reinforce points of interest for any state.

Courtesy of ActiveAcademics.org

PRESIDENTIAL RACE

Activity type: Physically active instruction—social studies

Target grades: 4-5

Equipment: A cutout of each U.S. state with the number of electoral votes written under that state name and three presidential name tags

Description: Ask for three volunteers to be the presidential candidates, and have them stand in the middle of the activity area. The rest of the class is assigned a state and instructed to line up (in a spread-out manner) at one end of the space. Each state name tag has a number under the state name that represents the number of electoral votes that state receives in an election. When the presidential candidates yell "The race is on," the states move (have students hop, skip, jump, etc.) past the candidates to the other end of the space without getting tagged by the candidates. When a state gets tagged, they belong to the candidate who tagged them. The state must then help its candidate capture more states until all states are captured. Each candidate and its group of states will then add up their electoral votes to determine who will be the next president of the United States. Afterward, discuss electoral votes, populations, and the importance of each state's vote. Sample questions include *Does it really matter which state each candidate wins in the electoral race? How many votes are necessary to win the electoral college?* and *Who won the election?*

Courtesy of ActiveAcademics.org

Summary

In physically active instruction, the teacher incorporates 11- to 30-minute bouts of fun physical activity into academic instruction. It can be done in the classroom or wherever the instruction takes place (indoors or outdoors), and it can be a part of any subject, including math, language arts, science, and social studies. Many physical activities can take place deskside or in open space in the classroom. Bouts of physical activity integrated into instruction have been shown to improve cognition, including attention, memory, general and verbal knowledge, processing speed, and executive control following exercise. Regular physical activity benefits the brain, cognition, and academic outcomes including academic achievement tests in preadolescent children.

CHAPTER 3

RECESS

Quick Start

- *What?* Recess is a regularly scheduled period within the school day for physical activity and play that is usually monitored by training staff or volunteers.

- *Why?* Participation in recess has cognitive, academic, social, emotional, and physical benefits for children. They need time to rest, play, imagine, think, move, and socialize (Council on School Health, 2013).

- *Where?* Recess traditionally takes place outdoors on the school grounds. If weather conditions are not suitable for outdoor play and physical activity, indoor options can be made available.

- *Who?* Recess is for all students, regardless of income, race, ethnicity, sex, gender identity, sexual identity, religion, physical or mental ability, appearance, or other characteristics (McMullen & Walton-Fisette, 2022).

- *How long?* National organizations recommend providing a starting duration of 20 minutes of recess daily for elementary students.

- *When?* Recess can be offered multiple times daily. Recess is not a replacement for physical education. Studies have shown that recess before lunch is optimal and recess after physical education is not optimal.

Quick Tips

- Consistently provide recess for all students.
- Offer recess in safe spaces outdoors.
- Supply loose equipment, such as balls, hoops, and skipping ropes, on the playground.
- Ensure that supervising adults are supportive and engaged in recess.
- Use or adapt the "54321" strategy (Heidorn & Heidorn, 2018):
  - 5: No more than five students are waiting in line to play a game or get equipment.

- 4: Think of four physically active things to do before recess starts. For example, students can turn to a peer and tell them what they plan to do as a ticket out the door.
- 3: Students are limited to three consecutive wins at a game before they need to move to another activity.
- 2: Restroom and water breaks are limited to two minutes.
- 1: Use one game of rock, paper, scissors to settle a game dispute.

Details

In addition to providing more detail about the benefits of recess, this section includes information you can share with administrators, other teachers and school staff, and parents.

Why Is This Important?

Recess has unique benefits during the school day. According to the American Academy of Pediatrics, it provides a break from rigorous cognitive tasks and is a time for children to play, rest, imagine, think, move, socialize, and develop social skills (Council on School Health, 2013).

Both the play and physical activity that are part of recess are beneficial. Extensive research shows that play enhances childhood development by fostering social-emotional, cognitive, language, and self-regulation skills, which build executive function and a prosocial brain. Indeed, play is not frivolous; it has positive effects on both brain structure and functioning. Other benefits of play are well documented; they include improvements in early math skills (numerosity and spatial concepts), social development, peer relations, physical development, and health, and enhanced sense of agency (Yogman et al., 2018).

Similarly, as presented in earlier chapters, moderate to vigorous physical activity has proven benefits. Performing bouts of moderate to vigorous physical activity improves attention, general and verbal knowledge, processing speed, and executive control during the period following the exercise (HHS, 2018). Long-term moderate to vigorous physical activity benefits the brain, cognition, and academic outcomes including performance on academic achievement tests in preadolescent children (HHS, 2018; Hillman et al., 2019). Research also shows that simply being outdoors increases physical activity in children (Gray et al., 2015; Brittin et al., 2015; Pate et al., 2019).

Many, but not all, children are physically active at recess. Boys are more active than girls, and younger students are more physically active than older students during recess. Many public health experts see recess as a time to promote physical activity more pointedly for all students. Interventions to promote physical activity at recess are often called *enhanced recess*. Enhanced recess interventions include

- providing structured and planned physical activity with a leader,
- supplying loose equipment for child play,
- changing the physical environment with playground markings,
- enhancing the social environment at recess with teacher training, and
- approaches that are combinations of these interventions (Parrish et al., 2020; Ridgers et al., 2020).

Accumulating research in this area indicates that these interventions show promise for increasing moderate to vigorous physical activity, but too few interventions exist in each category to assess evidence conclusively (Parrish et al., 2020; Pulido Sánchez et al., 2021; Ridgers et al., 2020). It is clear that adult encouragement and involvement are associated with reduced discipline problems, bullying, social exclusion, and social hierarchies among children, as well as increased physical activity on the playground (Massey et al., 2018; Massey et al., 2021).

The physical activity level of children at recess is influenced by many things, including the time allotted to recess; the size and quality of the space; the availability of fixed and loose equipment; the level of adult supervision, encouragement, and engagement; and the social environment on the playground (Massey et al., 2021; Ridgers et al., 2012). Lack of time (i.e., no recess or too little time at recess); small or poor-quality play spaces; lack of facilities and loose equipment such as balls and jump ropes; unengaged adults; and the presence of conflict, bullying, social exclusion, and social hierarchies (e.g., with larger groups of boys playing sports dominating facilities and marginalizing other students) reduce physical activity on the playground.

Each school is different. Schools differ in populations served, levels of resources including space and facilities, and recess policies and practices. Therefore, no one-size-fits-all approach exists for improving recess to provide your students with the full social-emotional, cognitive and academic, and health benefits of play and physical activity. Furthermore, making changes to recess is a schoolwide endeavor. The best approach to getting these benefits for your classroom is to plan specific strategies that work considering your school's specific situation. To be successful, planning for recess improvements should have support and involvement from school decision makers, key school personnel, parents, and students. As described in the section Carrying Out Recess, the CDC and SHAPE America (2017a, 2017b) provide guidance on enhancing elementary school recess.

How Much Is Enough?

CDC, SHAPE America, and other national organizations recommend a starting duration of 20 minutes for recess; that is, 20 minutes is not to be considered the maximum recommended time. Recess is distinct from physical education and other opportunities for physical activity during the school day. It should be for all children and should not be withheld for disciplinary reasons or for academic performance in the classroom. Do not use physical activity as punishment during recess (CDC and SHAPE America, 2017a).

What Principals, Teachers, and Parents Need to Know

Figure 3.1 summarizes the benefits of recess. Share this information with administrators, teachers, staff, parents, and others.

Carrying Out Recess

Following are some quick ideas to get started, followed by recommendations for enhancing the benefits of recess time for children.

Quick Ideas

- Provide a lot of loose equipment such as balls, hoops, and jump ropes. The more equipment they have available, the more students are engaged, and the more physical activity they get.
- Provide semistructured, optional opportunities for games or other physical activities with broad appeal during recess. Here are two examples:
  - Dance party: Put on some music and let the kids get their groove on to the beat of the music. Let the students play as usual for 5 to 10 minutes and introduce the dance party halfway through recess. The duration can be as short or as long as you like.
  - Track team: You (the teacher) run around on the playground, and the children follow you. The duration for this activity can also be as short or as long as you like.

Recommendations

Recess in a safe place with adult engagement is beneficial for children's social, emotional, cognitive, and physical development, but schools vary in their investment in recess time. Here are some recommendations to maximize recess for students in your school:

- Have recess lasting at least 20 minutes daily for all students.
- Adult support, engagement, and involvement in recess are important for social benefits and for maximizing physical activity during recess. Encourage your students to be physically active.

Benefits of Recess for Children

Provides a break and is a time to play, rest, imagine, think, move, socialize, and develop social skills

Fosters social–emotional, cognitive, language, and self-regulation skills

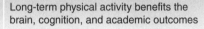

Physical activity improves attention, general and verbal knowledge, processing speed, and executive control after exercise

Long-term physical activity benefits the brain, cognition, and academic outcomes

Adult engagement in recess reduces conflict, bullying, and social exclusion

Enhanced recess has promise for promoting physical activity

Figure 3.1 Benefits of recess.

Information from HHS (2018); Hillman et al. (2019); Yogman et al. (2018); Council on School Health (2013); CDC and SHAPE America (2017a); Massey et al. (2018); Massey et al. (2021).

From R.R. Pate and R.P. Saunders, *Promoting Elementary School Physical Activity: Ideas for Enjoyable Active Learning* (Champaign, IL: Human Kinetics, 2024).

- For effective classroom management, have a plan for returning to class following recess. For example, use or adapt the so-called traffic light approach (Heidorn & Heidorn, 2018):
  - Green light: Be physically active as in outdoors at recess.
  - Yellow light: Tone activity levels down with slower movements, perhaps with calming music, such as in student-led stretching or a brief yoga session from a site such as GoNoodle.
  - Red light: Return to academic activities that are not physical.
- Structured physical activity interventions and changes to the playground to increase moderate to vigorous physical activity may be effective as part of an overall recess planning process such as that recommended by the CDC and SHAPE America. It is important to address both the social and physical environments on the playground. It is a schoolwide endeavor.

Fortunately, resources are available to assist your school with the recess planning process. The CDC and SHAPE America developed a guide called Strategies for Recess in Schools (CDC and SHAPE America, 2017a) to aid you in the planning process for improving recess in your school through five broad strategies. The guide provides specific steps, guidance, and options for each strategy, as summarized here:

1. *Make leadership decisions.* Strategies include identifying and documenting recess policies and putting them into practice, revising them as needed, developing a written recess plan, designating indoor and outdoor spaces for recess, establishing weather guidelines, and training school staff and volunteers for recess.

2. *Communicate and enforce behavioral and safety expectations.* Suggestions include developing and communicating behavior management strategies, teaching conflict resolution skills, and making sure that the space and facilities meet safety standards.

3. *Create an environment that is supportive of physical activity during recess.* Strategies include providing adequate equipment, creating physical activity zones with markings to delineate the playground, and providing planned physical activities.

4. *Engage the school community to support recess.* Strategies include defining roles and responsibilities of adult supervision of recess, involving students in planning and leading recess, and engaging parents and others to support school recess.

5. *Gather information on recess.* Suggestions include tracking physical activity during recess and gathering information to show the effects of recess on student and school outcomes.

Martinedoucet/E+/Getty Images

Children are naturally more active when they have space and spend time outdoors.

Schools can use the accompanying Recess Planning Template to facilitate the planning process for playground enhancement (CDC and SHAPE America, 2017b).

Children are more physically active when they are outdoors, which is an important reason for having recess outside, as well as having other outdoor physical activity opportunities at school. The next section presents important considerations for time spent outside of school buildings.

Considering the Outdoor Environment

Outdoor conditions vary from season to season and day to day, and the very best outdoor conditions are not always available. Even so, the range of safe conditions for outdoor physical activity is quite broad. However, weather, air quality, and solar radiation can sometimes present challenges to outdoor physical activity at school (Nathan et al., 2018). This section describes ways to address these possible challenges. It also covers a related issue, the importance of hydration in children and adolescents.

Weather and Air Quality

You cannot change the weather or the immediate air quality conditions. However, it is well within the reach of teachers and schools to have plans, policies, and practices in place to anticipate and navigate seasonal and daily fluctuations in weather and air quality. This preparation will help reduce children's exposure to unsafe or unhealthy conditions as well as enable you to take advantage of optimal outdoor conditions when they occur. School personnel can monitor the Air Quality Index (AQI), which reports daily air quality. The U.S. Environmental Protection Agency (EPA) calculates this index based on the levels of five major pollutants that are regulated by the Clean Air Act: ground-level ozone, particle pollution (also known as particulate matter), carbon monoxide, sulfur dioxide, and nitrogen dioxide. Air quality is closely associated with climate and weather patterns; in the United States, it is commonly reported with the weather.

Sun Safety

Teachers should be aware of the risks of skin cancer from high levels of exposure to ultraviolet radiation and sunburn, which is more likely at certain times of day and at certain times of the year. The amount of ultraviolet radiation one gets also depends on the latitude, altitude, climate, local weather, and pollution (Erem & Razzaque, 2021), and individuals differ in susceptibility to sunburn. Teachers also need to know that skin exposure to sunlight generates vitamin D, which is beneficial to health, especially bone health. Researchers have also identified other health benefits of sunlight (Alfredsson et al., 2020; Erem & Razzaque, 2021). Fortunately, the amount of sun exposure needed to produce vitamin D and health benefits is much less than the level that causes sunburn (Alfredsson et al., 2020). The UV index is a useful tool to help you plan for getting the benefits of sun exposure while minimizing the risks.

The National Weather Service calculates the ultraviolet (UV) index forecast for most zip codes across the United States, and the EPA publishes this information. The UV index forecasts the risk of overexposure to UV radiation from the sun, considering ozone depletion as well as seasonal and weather variations. The risk is reported a scale of 0 (low) to 11 or more (extremely high). Alerts may be issued for a particular area if the UV index is forecasted to be higher than usual. This information is useful for planning sun-safe activities outdoors.

The CDC also provides resources to help schools minimize excessive exposure to ultraviolet radiation at school (CDC, 2002). Recommendations include establishing policies that reduce exposure to ultraviolet radiation by extending or creating new shaded areas in commonly used outdoor areas; scheduling outdoor activities that avoid times of peak sun intensity; encouraging students to wear protective clothing, hats, and sunglasses; providing sun safety education for students and professional development for school staff; and informing and involving parents in sun safety for their children (CDC, 2002).

Hydration

According to expert studies, children and adolescents do not get sufficient hydration (Kenney et al., 2015; Khan et al., 2019). This condition may be worsened during periods of higher temperatures and increased physical activity (Bergeron, 2015). The body needs water for body systems to function, including the circulatory system, metabolism, temperature regulation, and water removal (Kenney et al., 2015). Excessive dehydration causes serious health problems, but even mild dehydration can cause headache, irritability, poorer physical performance, and reduced cognitive functioning in children and adults (Kenney et al., 2015). The negative effects of dehydration on cognitive function in children has been supported in studies (Khan et al., 2019; Merhej, 2018).

Fortunately, you can readily address dehydration simply with water intake (Khan et al., 2019; Merhej, 2018; Kenney et al., 2015). In children and adolescents, increasing water intake rather than other beverages including sports drinks appears to be more effective for hydration (Kenney et al., 2015; Bergeron, 2015). The CDC (2014) provides a comprehensive tool kit that enables schools to provide safe water for students.

Practical Strategies for Classroom Teachers

This section summarizes practical strategies that teachers and schools can consider to address challenges related to weather, air quality, sun safety, and hydration (Merhej, 2018). No single strategy works for every school in every location.

Weather, Air Quality, and Sun Safety

- Know your local climate, and monitor the weather, AQI, and UV index, all of which vary by time of day and season.
- Adjust scheduling within your power to take advantage of optimal outdoor conditions for outdoor activities.
- Have a plan A, plan B, and so on, as needed to address what you will do if inclement weather, poor air quality, or high levels of UV radiation prevent children from spending time outdoors. For example, you can lead fun physical activities in your classroom using *IDEAL* and other resources.
- Work with your school to prepare ahead of time for inclement weather, poor air quality, and overexposure to the sun.
  - Develop school policies and classroom practices that define safe weather and air quality conditions and that allow for sun safety, particularly during periods of higher UV radiation exposure.

- Develop school policies and classroom practices that provide alternative opportunities for physical activity when outdoor conditions are not suitable.
- Arrange alternative indoor spaces within the school if outdoor conditions are not favorable.
- Develop regular communication with parents concerning school policies and practices related to weather, air quality, and sun safety.
- Use the CDC's guidelines for preventing skin cancer (CDC, 2002).

Hydration

- Ensure that all children have access to safe drinking water throughout the school day.
- If you have vending machines or canteens, provide bottled water. Limit the availability of competitive sugar-sweetened beverages that are marketed in schools.
- Remind children to drink water (including in the classroom) and provide positive reinforcement for it.
- Educate students and parents on the benefits of hydration.
- Use the CDC's guidelines for increasing access to water in schools (CDC, 2014).

Ideas for Physically Active Recess

Table 3.1 presents some ideas that are great to use after children have settled into recess and need a little boost.

Table 3.1   Sample Physical Activities for Recess

Name	Grades	Location
Compliment Tag	K-3	Gym or outdoors
Can You . . .	K-3	Gym or outdoors
At the Race Track	K-3	Gym or outdoors
Balloon Keep-Up	K-5	Gym or outdoors
Fire Engine	K-5	Gym or outdoors
Loose Caboose	2-5	Gym or outdoors
Stomp and Shake	4-5	Gym or outdoors
Toss Up	4-5	Gym or outdoors
If, You Run	4-5	Gym or outdoors

COMPLIMENT TAG

Type: Recess

Target grades: K-3

Equipment: Items to identify taggers (e.g., ribbons, pinnies, gloves, bandanas, necklaces made of artificial flowers)

Description: Three to five participants volunteer to be taggers, which you identify with prepared markers. Participants move throughout the space trying to tag and to avoid being tagged. Tagged participants must freeze with one hand held high. To free a tagged player, a free player must high-five the frozen player's hand and offer a compliment. Change taggers often.

Tips: Ensure that the activity space is a safe distance from walls and free of hazards (e.g., benches, equipment, basketball nets, holes, loose gravel, wet grass); remove or mark any hazards. Remind participants to keep their heads up and to be aware of others when moving through the space.

Variations: To decrease the challenge,

- increase the size of the playing area.
- allow taggers to use an implement (e.g., pool noodle) to tag.

To increase the challenge,

- change the way the participants must travel (e.g., skip, gallop, hop).
- decrease the size of the playing area.

Adapted by permission from H. Gardner, *Physical Literacy on the Move. Games for Developing Confidence and Competence in Physical Activity* (Champaign, IL: Human Kinetics, 2017).

CAN YOU . . .

Type: Recess

Target grades: K-3

Equipment: None

Description: Participants scatter throughout the activity space. They perform the appropriate movement based on you asking them "Can you . . ."

- run quickly but softly in a straight line? In a curved line?
- hop sideways? To the left? To the right? Low to the ground?
- crawl close to the ground like a snake? Move forward? Move backward?
- gallop in a straight line while changing directions whenever you meet a classmate?
- fly like an airplane moving quickly in curved paths?
- walk tall like a long-legged clown on stilts? Walk backward?
- make your body wiggle like jelly? Wiggle only your hand? Arm? Belly? Leg?
- do a straight movement with your arms? Your knees? Your head?
- leap high over a rock? Long over a puddle? Quickly over a snake?
- gallop like a pony in a zigzag formation?
- walk slowly as if you have just landed on the moon? Walk on the moon sideways? Backward? In a curved formation?

Tips: Ensure that the activity space is a safe distance from hazards (e.g., walls, equipment, debris); remove or mark any hazards. Remind participants to keep their heads up and to be aware of others when moving through the space.

Variations: To decrease the challenge,

- have participants travel while moving fewer body parts.
- require only forward and backward movements.
- have participants reduce their speed while performing each activity.

To increase the challenge,

- require that participants move many body parts at once.
- have participants move at different heights.
- place participants in pairs or small groups.
- have participants use an implement (e.g., bounce a ball, balance a beanbag).

Adapted by permission from H. Gardner, *Physical Literacy on the Move. Games for Developing Confidence and Competence in Physical Activity* (Champaign, IL: Human Kinetics, 2017).

AT THE RACE TRACK

Type: Recess

Target grades: K-3

Equipment: None

Description: Participants are each assigned a type of vehicle (e.g., car, bus, motorcycle); each vehicle will have multiple participants. They begin standing in a circle; their place in the circle is called the *garage.* When you call out a vehicle, participants assigned that vehicle race around the circle clockwise and then back to their respective garages. If space permits, consider calling out "Rush hour," at which point all participants race around the circle to their garages.

Tips: Ensure that activity spaces are a safe distance from walls and free of hazards (e.g., benches, equipment, basketball nets, holes, loose gravel, wet grass); remove or mark any hazards. Remind participants to keep their heads up and to be aware of others when moving through the space.

Variations: To decrease the challenge, call only one or two vehicles to reduce the number of participants running at a time.

To increase the challenge,

- increase the size of the circle.
- add one participant in the center who joins each round and attempts to take other vehicles' garages by racing them around the circle.

Adapted by permission from H. Gardner, *Physical Literacy on the Move. Games for Developing Confidence and Competence in Physical Activity* (Champaign, IL: Human Kinetics, 2017).

BALLOON KEEP-UP

Type: Recess

Target grades: K-5

Equipment: One balloon for every two children, plus extra balloons inflated in case any pop during the game (Larger balloons work best because they stay in the air longer.)

Description: The children pair up, and each pair is given an inflated balloon. Their first goal is to see if they can throw or tap the balloon back and forth to each other, with each partner catching and throwing or hitting the balloon once. Then ask players to see if (or how long) they can tap the balloon back and forth without letting it fall to the floor or ground. If the balloon touches the floor or ground, they just pick it up and begin tapping it back and forth again. Kids love to do this simple cooperative activity, which introduces the idea of a common goal and the importance of taking turns.

Variations: For an additional challenge for preschoolers, Balloon Keep-Up can be played in groups of three. Three children try to keep one balloon in the air, with each taking a turn. Another fun option is to give each child a balloon. Partners sit (or stand) facing each other, and both children throw their own balloons into the air at about the same time; they try to catch their partner's balloon before it touches the ground. Then they repeat the balloon exchange process.

For an additional challenge, older children can count the number of consecutive hits before the balloon touches the floor or play the game in small groups of three or four, with each child taking a turn, while in different formations (e.g., circle, square).

For a cooperative challenge without a score, partners or groups of three can work together to keep a balloon in the air with alternating hand hits while moving from one end of the play area to the other or while going through an obstacle course (e.g., over walls, through tunnels, and so on). They can also attempt to keep a balloon up outdoors in the wind or rain or with the aid of an implement such as a paper plate or cardboard fan.

Adapted by permission from T. Orlick, *Cooperative Games and Sports,* Second Edition. (Champaign, IL: Human Kinetics, 2006).

FIRE ENGINE

Type: Recess

Target grades: K-5

Equipment: Any arbitrary object to indicate the fire

Description: Divide the group into lines of five or six participants. Have groups make parallel lines facing in the same direction. Set up the imaginary fire about 50 feet (15 m) in front of the line. Send the first person in each line (*fire engine*) to put the fire out. The participants indicate sirens with their voices and flashing lights with an arm flailing over the head. When an engine gets to the fire, that participant becomes a fire fighter holding a fire hose and shooting water on the fire.

It turns out to be a big fire, so the first engine goes back to the line to get a second engine from their own line, both of whom are wailing and flailing the whole time. They both race off, holding hands to put out the fire. This action repeats until every person in each line has been fetched.

As fire engines rush back and forth, they need to be careful not to crash into one another. A friendly reminder should take care of it, but if the activity becomes unsafe, stop all action to make sure it is addressed. One solution is to move the groups farther apart. You can always ask the participants for ideas on making it safer.

Variations: Vary the distance to the fire.

Adapted by permission from D.N. Le Fevre, *Best New Games,* Updated Edition (Champaign, IL: Human Kinetics, 2012).

LOOSE CABOOSE

Type: Recess

Target grades: 2-5

Equipment: None

Description: Clearly define the playing area. Have participants get into groups of three. At least three trains each with one caboose are needed. If students remain, they will become loose cabooses. If everyone is in a group of three, ask one group to become the loose cabooses. Make sure you have a loose caboose for every two or three trains. Each group of three will form a train, with one person behind another. The person behind places both hands on the shoulders of the person in front.

When you say "Start," the trains chug at a brisk pace that keeps the train connected around the area, and the loose cabooses quickly seek a train to join. This means that they attach to the last person in the train by taking hold of the person's shoulders. When they do so, they yell, "Go!" This is the signal for the engine (the first person in the train) to disconnect, thereby becoming a loose caboose. The trains move, trying to dodge the loose cabooses. The game goes on until players start to tire, about a few minutes.

All players need to remain aware of one another. When moving to avoid a caboose, the train may crash into another train, possibly hurting players. If it becomes a problem, slow down the locomotion of the players (e.g., by walking).

Adapted by permission from D.N. Le Fevre, *Best New Games,* Updated Edition (Champaign, IL: Human Kinetics, 2012).

STOMP AND SHAKE

Type: Recess

Target grades: 4-5

Equipment: One jump rope or similar length of rope for every two children

Description: The students are divided into two groups: shakers and stompers. The shakers each hold one end of an 8-foot (2.5 m) rope between the thumb and first finger and wiggle the rope so that the other end drags along the ground or floor. When the game starts, shakers run around the play area, shaking the rope on the ground or floor behind them. The stompers run after the shakers and try to step on the end of one of the ropes, which usually pulls it loose from between the shaker's fingers. Once a stomper has stepped on a rope and it has fallen to the ground or floor, the stomper picks it up and becomes a shaker. The shaker who just dropped the rope becomes a stomper, so their roles are reversed.

Tip: To keep the game moving, you may need to start with a few more stompers than shakers.

Adapted by permission from T. Orlick, *Cooperative Games and Sports,* Second Edition. (Champaign, IL: Human Kinetics, 2006).

TOSS UP

Type: Recess

Target grades: 4-5

Equipment: Five or six plush objects per group

Description: Divide participants into teams of six to eight, which then pair up to compete. Each pair begins with one plush object. When you say "Toss up," a participant on one team throws the object straight up about 8 to 10 feet (2.5-3.0 m), and that team performs a task together and in sync (e.g., jumping jack, squat, calf raise); they count the repetitions out loud until the object is caught or retrieved by someone on the other team, who then shouts "Stop."

The throwing group receives points for the number of times they performed the task (e.g., 10 jumping jacks = 10 points). If the object was caught before hitting the ground or floor, a second object is added. The activity is repeated, this time with the other team throwing two objects at the same time. Both objects need to be caught or retrieved by the other team to stop the group from collecting points. If both objects are caught before hitting the ground or floor, a third object is added, and the game continues. If both objects are not caught, then the game continues with only two objects.

Tips: Ensure that the activity space is a safe distance from walls and free of hazards (e.g., benches, equipment, basketball nets, holes, loose gravel, wet grass); remove or mark any hazards. Provide safe distances between games occurring in the same space. Remind participants to keep their heads up and to be aware of others when moving through the space.

Variations: To decrease the challenge,

- reduce the required height of the throw.
- allow groups to choose which members will catch and which members will perform the physical task.
- use objects that are easier to catch (e.g., larger or brighter, with handles to grab).

To increase the challenge,

- increase the required height of the throw.
- decrease the size of the object.
- use objects that are more difficult to catch (e.g., rubber chickens, objects with uneven weighting).

Adapted by permission from H. Gardner, *Physical Literacy on the Move. Games for Developing Confidence and Competence in Physical Activity* (Champaign, IL: Human Kinetics, 2017).

IF, YOU RUN

Type: Recess

Target grades: 4-5

Equipment: None

Description: Participants form a large circle and jog in place. One person is in the center and calls out a yes–no question (e.g., "Are you wearing blue?" "Did you have cereal for breakfast?" "Do you know how to ice skate?"). Participants who answer yes must leave their spots and run around the circle before returning to their spots. The questioner joins the group running around the circle and attempts to take someone's place in the circle. If the questioner succeeds, the misplaced person becomes the questioner. Change questioners often.

Tips: Ensure that the activity space is a safe distance from walls and free of hazards (e.g., benches, equipment, basketball nets, holes,

loose gravel, wet grass); remove or mark any hazards. Remind participants to keep their heads up and to be aware of others when running
around the circle.

Variations: To decrease the challenge,

- decrease the size of the circle.
- have participants run with a partner.
- require that participants walk around the circle.

To increase the challenge, increase the size of the circle.

Adapted by permission from H. Gardner, *Physical Literacy on the Move. Games for Developing Confidence and Competence in Physical Activity* (Champaign, IL: Human Kinetics, 2017).

Summary

Recess is a regularly scheduled period for physical activity and play within the school day. It is usually monitored by training staff or volunteers. National organizations recommend providing a starting duration of 20 minutes of recess daily for elementary students, and recess can be offered multiple times a day. It traditionally takes place outdoors on the school grounds. If weather conditions are not suitable for outdoor play and physical activity, indoor options can be made available. Recess has cognitive, academic, social, emotional, and physical benefits for children. They need time to rest, play, imagine, think, move, and socialize. Recess is for all students, regardless of income, race, ethnicity, sex, gender identity, sexual identity, religion, physical or mental ability, appearance, or other characteristics.

CHAPTER 4

THE PHYSICALLY ACTIVE CLASSROOM

Quick Start

- *What?* Classrooms that combine nontraditional arrangements of furniture and space with student-centered learning reduce barriers to physical activity. Adding opportunities for classroom physical activity in both nontraditional and traditional classrooms helps children become even more physically active.

- *Why?* Together and separately, nontraditional spaces and student-centered learning as well as physical activity opportunities in the classroom result in students who are healthier, are more engaged, feel a sense of belonging, and perform better academically.

- *Where?* The *physically active classroom* means the classroom that supports physical activity. It includes the physical space and arrangement of furniture, the teaching approach and instructional methods, and the classroom social environment.

- *Who and when?* The physically active classroom benefits all who spend time in the classroom space, and it has positive effects the whole time they are there in class.

Details

In addition to providing more details on the elements of a physically active classroom, this section includes information on benefits of a physically active classroom to share with principals, teachers, parents, and others.

What Is a Physically Active Classroom?

A physically active classroom is a place that makes both learning and physical activity easy and natural. It includes three elements (figure 4.1):

- Nontraditional spaces with student-centered learning approaches

59

- An emphasis on promoting choice, mastery, and a sense of belonging for student learning
- A provision of physical activity opportunities in the classroom

Nontraditional spaces and student-centered learning contribute to less sitting and more moving in class. They are consistent with social norms that facilitate implementing many of the physical activity recommendations for children in *IDEAL* and other resources. Preliminary evidence indicates that children are less sedentary and more physically active in these settings (Byun et al., 2013; Pate et al., 2014; Kariippanon et al., 2021). Promoting choice, mastery, and a sense of belonging in the classroom is consistent with the student-centered approach to learning and builds a positive motivational climate for students.

Providing fun and engaging physical activity opportunities during the school day also contributes to a physically active classroom. Earlier chapters in *IDEAL* as well as other resources suggest ideas for physically active opportunities including classroom breaks, physical activity integrated into instruction, and school recess breaks. These opportunities contribute to children's physical activity in both traditional and nontraditional classrooms, although nontraditional classrooms seem to have fewer challenges. Each of the elements contributing to a physically active classroom are discussed in the following sections.

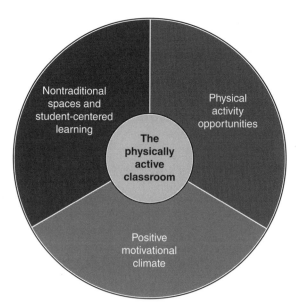

Figure 4.1 Three elements of a physically active classroom.

Nontraditional Spaces With Student-Centered Learning Approaches

This element of a physically active classroom has two components: the arrangement of furniture and classroom space, and student-centered (rather than teacher-directed) learning.

Arrangement of Furniture and Classroom Space   Classroom space and how it is arranged affects learning, student performance, and well-being (Kariippanon et al., 2018). Flexible arrangements have a variety of furniture options in a relatively open space that can be configured in multiple ways. These spaces can support both individual and collaborative work and may use a range of technologies for personalized learning (Kariippanon et al., 2018). This arrangement contrasts with the traditional positioning of the teacher in the front of the room facing the students, who sit in rows of desks and remain seated for long periods. Nontraditional spaces enable children and adults to move around throughout the day, and they may provide open space for physical activity. They are often associated with student-centered learning.

In 2015, Brittin and colleagues published "Physical Activity Design Guidelines for School Architecture," a set of comprehensive guidelines for designing school environments that are more conducive to physical activity. Based on a review of 77 studies, they provided recommendations for the design and renovation of classrooms. They found emerging evidence related to designing classrooms that promote physical activity as follows:

- Provide ample room for children and teachers to move in the classroom, supporting physical activity breaks as well as physical activity programs.
- Provide a flexible class layout for multiple and changing configurations.

In addition, several best practices with promise for promoting physical activity were identified as follows:

- Design modular areas and learning hubs, including activity and reading nooks.
- Allow space for student-defined learning areas.
- Provide easy access from classrooms to outdoor play and learning areas, especially for younger children.

Student-Centered Approaches to Learning   In student-centered approaches, students are central to their own learning (Kariippanon et al., 2018). This concept contrasts the familiar approach of teacher-directed learning. Baeten and colleagues (2016) present five design principles for student-centered learning environments, and Kariippanon and colleagues (2018) provide examples of teaching and learning activities as well as the types of spaces in which they can take place. These principles and examples are presented as follows:

- Students construct knowledge by actively participating in their learning—selecting, interpreting, and applying new information. This approach contrasts with the teacher simply providing the target information.
  - Teaching and learning activities include project-based learning, direct instruction, research-based learning, reflective activities, and discussion.
  - These activities can take place in group learning areas, in breakout spaces, in individual pods, and with technology.
- Teachers become facilitators of learning by stimulating students through open-ended questions and providing hints when students become stuck.
  - Teaching and learning activities include collaborative and group work, reflective activities, and discussion.
  - The classroom has no distinct front of the classroom, and learning may take place in group learning and breakout areas.
- Students learn in cooperation with other students in heterogeneous and small groups. Kariippanon and colleagues (2018) note that options for individual work are also important.
  - Teaching and learning strategies include collaborative and group work and peer-to-peer learning. Learning takes place in group learning areas, in breakout and presentation spaces, and with access to technology.
- Assignments are authentic, relating to real-life situations; for example, work may be project based, case based, or inquiry based.
  - Teaching and learning strategies include project- and research-based learning. They may take place through one-on-one teacher–student conferencing and in individual pods, group learning areas, and presentation spaces.
- Opportunities for self-regulated learning are part of the learning environment. For example, students have choices about working individually or in groups, in different spaces, and with technology. They become more engaged, motivated, and independent by setting goals, making plans, and carrying them out.
  - Teaching and learning strategies include self-directed learning, peer-to-peer learning, and reflective work, and they take place in individual pods and group learning areas.

The teacher values and has positive expectations for each child, which helps to create the child's sense of belonging to a community. In a facilitative role, teachers structure classroom experiences and engage in behaviors that encourage students to make personal choices, build a sense of mastery, and develop satisfying social relationships. The consistency between flexible learning approaches and tenets of self-determination theory have been noted, particularly the emphasis on student autonomy (choice), mastery, and supportive relationships (Kariippanon et al., 2018; Lillard, 2019).

Choice, Mastery, and Supportive Relationships for Learning

Having choices, developing mastery, and forming positive student-to-student and student-to-teacher relationships are core concepts from self-determination theory (Kariippanon et al., 2018; Baeten et al., 2016; Ryan & Deci, 2000). These three elements address innate human needs; they suggest that people naturally strive for autonomy (in which behavior is a personal choice), competence (in which one has a sense of mastery), and relatedness (in which relationships are supportive) (Ryan & Deci, 2000).

The Montessori approach to education embodies many of the principles of flexible learning spaces, student-centered learning, and concepts from self-determination theory including choice, mastery, and supportive social environments (Lillard, 2019). In Montessori education, children work in flexible spaces and interact freely with their peers, which addresses the need for belonging and relatedness. Children develop a sense of autonomy by choosing among opportunities for many hands-on activities, which help develop a sense of competence or mastery. As a facilitator of learning, the teacher prepares the environment and materials ahead of time so that children can choose freely within an ordered and structured environment that supports each child's learning (Lillard, 2019).

Physical Activity Opportunities in the Classroom

IDEAL presents tips, strategies, and ideas for providing physical activity opportunities during the school day, including classroom physical activity breaks (chapter 1), physical activity integrated into instruction (chapter 2), and school recess breaks (chapter 3). Later chapters present other ways to provide physical activity opportunities before, during, and after the school day (chapters 5, 6, and 7). Providing opportunities for physical activity at school is an effective approach for increasing children's physical activity in traditional classrooms as well as nontraditional spaces and student-centered learning classrooms. Nontraditional spaces and student-centered learning classrooms seem to have fewer challenges in carrying out physical activities in class; for example, these spaces may have more open areas in the room in which children can be active.

Why Is This Important?

The nontraditional arrangement of furniture and space works together with student-centered learning approaches to benefit teaching and learning as well as the students' social, emotional, and physical well-being (Kariippanon et al., 2018). Kaput (2018) documented many benefits for each of the principles of student-centered learning, including student ownership and agency (students have freedom to exercise choice in pursuing interests with teachers serving as guides and facilitators) and positive relationships (students have relationships with adults and peers who care about, believe in, and hold them to high expectations).

For example, students engaged in project-based learning had higher gains on standardized tests compared to peers in traditional schools, and positive peer relationships were important for students' personal growth; academic success; and cognitive, social, and language development (Kaput, 2018). A review of the limited number of studies available (six) found promising evidence that flexible learning spaces resulted in improvements in behavioral cognitive outcomes and engagement, positive student-to-student interaction, and better academic outcomes in English, mathematics, and humanities (Kariippanon et al., 2021).

Approaches based on supporting students' need for autonomy (choice), competence (mastery), and supportive relationships (a sense of belonging) are more effective for learning than those that are based on external controls, monitoring, and evaluation. Controlling conditions tend to take away feelings of interest, enjoyment, and enthusiasm, and external rewards motivate only in the short run. Consistent research has shown that teaching that supports student autonomy improves students' intrinsic motivation and performance in school (Niemiec & Ryan, 2009).

Similarly, a comprehensive review found evidence that children may benefit cognitively and socially from Montessori education that follows its creator's principles (Marshall, 2017). Studies in non-Montessori classrooms that have adopted Montessori elements provide support for specific components of the Montessori approach. These elements include the use of Montessori practical materials that develop children's fine motor skills and attention; the Montessori approach to early literacy through phonics; and its sensorial approach for providing a foundation in mathematics (Marshall, 2017).

A review of flexible learning spaces (Kariippanon et al., 2021) found preliminary evidence that students move around more in flexible learning environments with reduced sedentary time and increased standing and stepping during lessons. Similarly, although Montessori was developed as an educational and learning approach, it also creates a physical and social environment that is more conducive to movement than traditional classrooms. This environment may result in more physical activity, as was shown in studies in which children attending Montessori preschools were less sedentary and more physically active than children in traditional preschools (Byun et al., 2013; Pate et al., 2014).

Together and separately, nontraditional spaces with student-centered learning approaches and physical activity opportunities in the classroom result in students who are healthier, are more engaged, feel a sense of belonging, and perform better academically. As discussed in the following sections, many of the strategies that make student-centered learning an effective approach for education can be used to make physical activity engaging, fun, and relevant for students.

What Principals, Teachers, and Parents Need to Know

Figure 4.2 summarizes the benefits of physically active classrooms that have a flexible, open physical environment and student-centered approach to learning. Share this information with administrators, teachers, staff, parents, and others.

Carrying Out Nontraditional Space and Student-Centered Learning Approaches

The (Not So) Quick Tips section succinctly summarizes the processes involved in implementing flexible learning spaces in the classroom. Things to Consider describes the processes of changing to flexible learning spaces that combine nontraditional spaces and student-centered learning approaches.

(Not So) Quick Tips

- Changing the classroom space without changing the traditional teaching approach will not produce the benefits of nontraditional spaces plus student-centered learning.
- Changing to nontraditional arrangements of furniture and space in classrooms along with adopting a student-centered approach to learning requires full buy-in, commitment, and participation from administrators and teachers.
  - Open communication is essential.
  - It is important to involve students and parents.
  - Change is facilitated by an internal champion.
- Organizational change is a process that can be phased in over time.
- Professional development and ongoing support are essential.

Benefits of Physically Active Classrooms

Physical activity opportunities in class add to daily physical activity

Flexible learning spaces benefit students' social, emotional, and physical well-being

Physical activity in class improves
- Time on task
- Attentiveness
- Academic outcomes

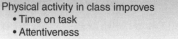

The arrangement of classroom furniture and space affects learning, student performance, and well-being

Students in flexible learning spaces sit less and move more

Physical activity
- Improves health and fitness
- Develops motor skills that support lifelong physical activity
- Helps form healthy habits for a lifetime

Flexible learning spaces improve
- Behavioral cognitive outcomes
- Engagement
- Positive student-to-student interaction
- Academic outcomes

Figure 4.2 Benefits of physically active classrooms.

Information from HHS (2018); Norris et al. (2020); Hillman et al. (2019); Kariippanon et al. (2018 & 2021); Byun et al. (2013); Pate et al. (2014).

From R.R. Pate and R.P. Saunders, *Promoting Elementary School Physical Activity: Ideas for Enjoyable Active Learning* (Champaign, IL: Human Kinetics, 2024).

Things to Consider

To create the physical environment for flexible learning spaces in the classroom, remove rows of desks and chairs. Replace them with a range of comfortable furniture items (that vary by grade level) arranged in a variety of ways within in a comparatively open space. This more flexible space may feature a range of technologies and can facilitate a variety of teaching and learning experiences that offer individual and collaborative work (Kariippanon et al., 2020).

Additional funds are not always needed to change a traditional elementary classroom structure into a more flexible learning space (Kariippanon et al., 2020). Depending on school resources, classroom configurations may include the following:

- Arranging tables and chairs that seat small numbers of students around the edges of the room
- Having soft, low chairs, stools, or bean bags clustered in an area
- Creating secluded spaces for individual work
- Having standing writing tables in a space
- Placing rugs or mats on the floor to define spaces
- Buying specialized furniture and equipment

Most flexible learning spaces strive to keep open space in the room.

Simply changing the classroom into a more flexible configuration is not enough to result in changes to teaching and learning. Rather, it is important to simultaneously strive to change teaching practices to get the benefits of both nontraditional arrangements of furniture and space and student-centered learning (Kariippanon et al., 2020).

Changing to nontraditional spaces and student-centered learning ideally has both top–down and bottom–up commitments; that is, both the head administrator and the teachers need to be on board to create the momentum needed to change. In eight schools in Australia, the commitment to nontraditional spaces and student-centered learning came with the broad commitment to moving away from didactic teaching and toward a more student-centered approach and the belief in the benefits of making these challenging changes (Kariippanon et al., 2020). Making this change is ideally a choice that teachers make rather than a requirement that is forced on them (Kariippanon et al., 2020).

Getting input from everyone (including teaching staff, students, and community) through an open and systematic process is important to success. For example, elementary students participated by building cardboard box models of how they saw the ideal learning space (Kariippanon et al., 2020). Organizational change needs internal champions, enthusiastic people who support the cause. A principal may champion the transformation, but the champion could be a classroom teacher, especially in elementary school. It is important to consider the unique needs of each school when making decisions about furniture and resources (Kariippanon et al., 2020).

Change is a process that takes time and can be done in phases. All classrooms do not have to change at the same time. For example, the process can begin with two teachers who are already committed to the need for change. Phasing in the change enables these teachers to try out the environmental and teaching changes and make modifications as needed. In addition, it allows other teachers who are less comfortable with flexible spaces and student-centered learning to see the space in action before jumping into it (Kariippanon et al., 2020).

Even teachers who are fully on board with the changes will need professional development and ongoing support to ensure that flexible learning spaces are used optimally and sustained over time. Teachers also benefit from sharing their experiences with each other early and throughout the change process (Kariippanon et al., 2020).

According to Kariippanon and colleagues (2018), implementing something new always creates new challenges that can be overcome; challenges are part of the process of change. For example, one of the surmountable challenges teachers experienced with switching to nontraditional spaces and student-centered learning was students becoming more easily distracted in flexible spaces; staying on topic while discussing

Westend61/Getty Images

Nontraditional classrooms have open spaces that make providing physical activity easier.

with peers requires some skills that students need to develop. It is part of the teacher's role to help students stay on task. Another challenge of flexible learning spaces can be noise resulting from the relatively open spaces and multiple activities happening simultaneously. Teachers also found that setting classroom expectations and boundaries around using the space and furniture was needed to facilitate classroom management (Kariippanon et al., 2018).

Carrying Out Concepts Supporting Choice, Mastery, and Sense of Belonging

This section focuses on applying concepts from self-determination theory to nontraditional spaces and student-centered learning. (Not So) Quick Tips provides a brief summary, which is expanded with examples in Things to Consider.

(Not So) Quick Tips

- Compared to traditional teaching, emphasizing student choice, mastery, and sense of belonging requires a different mindset, different teaching strategies, and a new set of behaviors.
- The devil is in the details, and the small details often come down to verbal and nonverbal behavior between the teacher and the student.
- To change from traditional teaching approaches, teachers need administrative and peer support, especially to address external pressure emphasizing standardized testing.

Things to Consider

Students are intrinsically motivated to learn; they are naturally curious and interested. Teachers can work with these tendencies by supporting students' need for choice, mastery, and sense of belonging (Niemiec & Ryan, 2009). Providing choices and being less controlling doesn't mean that students can do anything they like. Setting limits is important in educational and other settings. Limits can be set in an informational manner that supports student autonomy rather than in a controlling manner that stifles it. This example of explaining painting a picture to a child shows an informational approach that supports student autonomy:

> Before you begin, I want to tell you some things about the way painting is done here. I know that sometimes it's really fun to just slop the paint around, but here the materials and room need to be kept nice for the other children who will use them. The smaller sheet is for you to paint on, the larger sheet is a border to be kept clean. Also,

the paints need to be kept clean, so the brush is to be washed and wiped in the paper towel before switching colors. I know that some kids don't like to be neat all the time, but now is a time for being neat (Koestner et al., 1984, p. 239).

This example of explaining painting a picture to a child shows a controlling approach that is less supportive of student autonomy:

Before you begin, I want to tell you some things that you will have to do. They are rules that we have about painting. You have to keep the paints clean. You can paint only on this small sheet of paper, so don't spill any paint on the big sheet. And you must wash out your brush and wipe it with a paper towel before you switch to a new color of paint, so that you don't get the colors all mixed up. In general, I want you to be a good boy (girl) and don't make a mess with the paints (Koestner et al., 1984, p. 239).

Teachers can support student autonomy by minimizing coercion and the importance of evaluation and by maximizing students' voices and choices in their academic activities. It is also helpful to explain to students why a learning activity is useful. Students' competence can be developed by providing them with learning activities that are in the so-called Goldilocks zone. Tasks are not too easy and not too hard; they are just right in the level of challenge to allow them to expand in their learning (Niemiec & Ryan, 2009).

Students also need task-specific feedback that supports their efforts and helps them master the material while downplaying evaluation and judgment of their performance. Finally, having a sense of belonging helps students become more intrinsically motivated; people tend to accept the values and practices of groups to which they belong (or to which they want to belong). If the teacher likes, respects, and values a student, then that student will be more involved in learning. Students who feel disconnected are more likely to respond only to external controls (Niemiec & Ryan, 2009).

Not all learning tasks may be intrinsically motivating for all students; that is, everything is not inherently interesting or fun in an immediate sense. In these situations, students may need another incentive. However, not all external incentives are created equal, and some approaches are more supportive of student autonomy than others. For example, students might want to master a difficult or tedious topic or task because it helps them achieve a future goal or to accomplish something that has personal value or meaning to them. Motivations that are less supportive of autonomy are to work to get a reward, avoid punishment, avoid feeling guilty, or not look bad to their peers (Niemiec & Ryan, 2009).

Teachers may use controlling approaches to instruction in the classroom because teachers themselves are subjected to external pressures concerning curricula and standardized test scores from the school, district, and higher levels. This external pressure does not support the teachers' sense of autonomy, competence, and relatedness. However, enlightened decision makers and like-minded, supportive peers can buffer these external influences on teachers to support teachers who would like to use student-centered approaches (Niemiec & Ryan, 2009).

Creating Physical Activity Opportunities in the Classroom

This section provides more ideas beyond those presented in earlier chapters for engaging children in physical activity in the classroom. It looks at the importance of space in the classroom and the usefulness of applying concepts from self-determination theory to involve children in physical activity. Quick Tips provides the overview, and Things to Consider provides more information for creating motivational physical activity environments.

Quick Tips

- To the extent possible, make space for physical activity in your classroom.
- Over time, establish routines that include regular physical activity opportunities for students through physical activity breaks, physically active instruction, physically active transitions, and regular recess.
- Strive to make physical activity fun with enthusiasm, variety, and music.
- Emphasize participation and effort over winning or performance; avoid competition.
- Encourage children to choose, lead, and invent physical activities.
- Adjust physical activities to include everyone and avoid elimination games.

Things to Consider

The Supportive, Active, Autonomous, Fair, and Enjoyable (SAAFE) teaching principles (Lubans et al., 2017) address motivational climate as part of the strategy for promoting moderate to vigorous physical activity in children in physical education as well as other exercise settings. SAAFE is discussed further in part II. Here is a summary of the SAAFE strategies that apply to elementary classroom teachers (adapted from Lubans et al., 2017):

- *Supportive.* Teachers can carry out even more effective classroom physical activity breaks and physically active instruction by providing a supportive environment that cultivates feelings of autonomy, competence, and social cohesion. Supportive teachers take the perspective of their students, provide explanations for what they are doing, use language that is not strict or controlling, and demonstrate emotional support. In contrast, a performance climate focuses on superior performance or winning.

- *Active.* Teachers can promote moderate to vigorous physical activity by having all students moving, avoiding elimination games, integrating high-intensity bursts of physical activity, and encouraging physical activity during transitions.

- *Autonomous.* Teachers can provide students choices of physical activities, involve them in creation and modification of activities and rules, and explain the reasoning for the different activities.

- *Fair.* Teachers can ensure all students have opportunities to experience success by minimizing competition, creating similar grouping of children for certain physical activities (as applicable), modifying activities to level the playing field, and structuring physical activities for enjoyment and participation rather than peer comparison or competition.

- *Enjoyable.* Teachers can design physical activities in which students have choice, feel competent, and interact with others to feel socially connected. Other strategies to create enjoyment include providing variety in activities and equipment, using activities that students like, and using appealing music.

Summary

The arrangement of classroom furniture to create open spaces that encourage movement and interaction, along with a student-centered approach to learning, feeds into a supportive classroom culture of belonging, involvement, and learning. It also supports increased movement. Providing fun physical activity opportunities such as physical activity breaks and physically active instruction using student-centered, supportive, and motivational strategies creates a culture of physical activity, which further enhances belonging, involvement, and learning. Seek administrative, peer, and professional development support as needed to facilitate developing a more physically active classroom.

Part II

PHYSICAL EDUCATION

Part II is written for the elementary physical education teacher. The two chapters in this section are designed to build on the traditional focus on instruction to create a physical education classroom that promotes moderate to vigorous physical activity, has a positive motivational climate, and makes connections to physical activity beyond the physical education classroom.

Chapter 5 (Enhanced Physical Education) focuses on increasing the amount of time children participate in moderate to vigorous physical activity during physical education class. The approaches and strategies of enhanced physical education include improved class organization, management, and instruction; supplementing standard physical education classes with high-intensity activity (fitness infusion); and striving to create or enhance positive motivational climates in physical education. It includes sample activities to use in physical education class.

Chapter 6 (Physical Education Beyond the Gymnasium) provides practical strategies for developing motivated students who want to be active outside of physical education class, connecting them to physical activity opportunities outside of physical education, and communicating with families and community organizations, the gatekeepers of children's physical activity.

CHAPTER 5
ENHANCED PHYSICAL EDUCATION

Quick Start

- *What?* Enhanced physical education involves curricula and practice-based approaches to increase the amount of time students engage in moderate to vigorous physical activity during physical education classes. Effective strategies include improved class organization, management, and instruction; supplementing standard physical education classes with high-intensity activity; and incorporating motivational elements in teaching physical education.

- *Why?* Engaging in moderate to vigorous physical activity is associated with numerous physical, mental, and cognitive benefits for children, and participating in enhanced physical education increases the percentage of time that students spend in moderate to vigorous physical activity. In addition, enhanced physical education has been shown to improve children's health-related physical fitness components, fundamental motor skills, and mental and emotional well-being.

- *Where?* Physical education typically takes place in a gymnasium and outdoors.

- *Who?* Physical education is ideally taught by certified physical education specialists. Classes should include all students of all abilities, backgrounds, and appearances, and teachers should adapt physical activities and instruction as needed for students with special needs or disabilities.

- *How long?* Physical education instructional time should total to a minimum of 150 minutes per week (30 minutes/day) in elementary schools. Students should spend at least 50 percent of class time in moderate to vigorous physical activity.

- *When?* Physical education is ideally scheduled daily for at least 30 minutes per class.

Details

In addition to outlining the benefits of enhanced physical education in more depth, this section includes information you can share with principals, teachers, parents, and others.

What Is Enhanced Physical Education?

In addition to its focus on physical education instruction, enhanced physical education strives to increase the amount of time children participate in moderate to vigorous physical activity during physical education class. The approaches and strategies of enhanced physical education include improved class organization, management, and instruction; supplementing standard physical education classes with high-intensity activity (fitness infusion); and striving to create or enhance positive motivational climates in physical education (figure 5.1) (Lonsdale et al., 2013; Wong et al., 2021).

Class Organization, Management, Instruction, and Fitness Infusion

Strategies that focus on improving class organization, management, and instruction and on supplementing standard physical education classes with high-intensity activity (fitness infusion) work with existing elements

Figure 5.1   Elements of enhanced physical education.

of most physical education classes. For example, teachers can streamline transitions, eliminate standing in lines, remove sitting, modify games, select games that are more active, intersperse brief high-intensity activities, and avoid elimination of physical activity in games to make the most of the limited physical education time (Lonsdale et al., 2013).

Class Motivational Environment

Strategies addressing motivational climate in physical education focus on meeting students' needs for autonomy, competence, and relatedness. Autonomy is the need to experience a sense of willingness in one's actions; competence refers to the need to experience effectiveness in one's interactions in the world; and relatedness is the need to be connected with significant others and to feel accepted (Vasconcellos et al., 2020). This approach differs greatly from traditional physical education classrooms. Traditional classrooms often are teacher directed rather than student oriented, with few opportunities for student choices; are performance oriented, with emphasis on competition and winning rather than mastery, participation, and self-improvement; and feature little social interaction rather than emphasize positive relationships.

The benefits of classroom environments that provide children a sense of autonomy, opportunities to develop mastery, and a sense of belonging (Ryan & Deci, 2000; Niemiec & Ryan, 2009) were introduced in chapter 4. These concepts are part of self-determination theory, which describes how motivation develops and affects well-being. If students' basic needs for autonomy, mastery, and relatedness are met, they develop more intrinsic motivation.

Intrinsic motivation is internalized; it arises from within the individual. Students who are intrinsically motivated are engaged and stay focused on tasks because those tasks are naturally satisfying to them. When their basic needs are not fully met, people tend to regulate their behavior by controlled (external) means in order to gain external rewards or avoid punishment (Vasconcellos et al., 2020). Because these motivations are external, they control behavior only while they are in place.

Not all educational tasks are inherently interesting and valued (they are not intrinsically motivating), but they are still important for the student. Therefore, one of the tasks of instruction is to help students develop more internalized values. The more the instructional environment supports the basic needs for autonomy (choice), competence (mastery), and relatedness (belonging), the more internalized motivation is enhanced (Vasconcellos et al., 2020).

Why Is This Important?

Enhanced physical activity programs increase moderate to vigorous physical activity in physical education (Community Preventive Services

Task Force, 2013; HHS, 2018; Lonsdale et al., 2013; Wong et al., 2021). Enhanced physical education programs improve body mass index, body fat percentage, lean body mass percentage, cardiorespiratory fitness, and muscular strength (García-Hermoso et al., 2020), and they make substantial improvements in fundamental motor skills in children and adolescents (García-Hermoso et al., 2020; Lorås, 2020).

Motor competence is associated with positive health outcomes as children develop, including muscular strength and endurance, cardiorespiratory fitness, healthy weight status, and physical activity (Robinson et al., 2015). In addition, motor competence has a reciprocal relationship with physical activity and lifelong physical activity. In other words, higher levels of movement skills lead to higher levels of physical activity, which in turn lead to higher levels of movement competence (Gleddie & Morgan, 2021).

Creating positive motivational climates based on self-determination theory is widely and successfully used in physical education. It relates positively to cardiovascular fitness; knowledge of strength and conditioning; motor skill performance; intentions to be physically active in the future; concentration, positive affect, and preference for challenging tasks; and persistence and effort (Sun et al., 2017).

Physical education teachers have a large influence on students' perceptions of autonomy and competence, and both teachers and peers influence feelings of relatedness (Vasconcellos et al., 2020). Physical education environments that promote choice, mastery, and relatedness are important for children's motivation in elementary physical education and for their skill development, highlighting the important role of physical education teachers (de Bruijn et al., 2022).

In summary, research clearly shows these benefits for enhanced physical education:

- Increased percentage of time spent in moderate to vigorous physical activity
- Improved health-related physical fitness components
- Improved motor skills in children, which is crucial to children's physical, social, and cognitive development
- Enhanced mental and emotional well-being

As reviewed in previous chapters in this book, moderate to vigorous physical activity has these physical, mental, and cognitive benefits for children and adolescents:

- Improved cardiorespiratory fitness
- Stronger bones and muscles
- Healthier weight

- Reduced symptoms of anxiety and depression
- Reduced risk of developing health conditions such as heart disease, cancer, type 2 diabetes, high blood pressure, osteoporosis, and obesity
- Improved cognition, including attention, general and verbal knowledge, processing speed, and executive control
- Improved brain, cognitive, and academic outcomes, including performance on academic achievement tests

How Much Is Enough

Physical education instructional time should total to a minimum of 150 minutes per week (30 minutes/day) in elementary schools. The goal in enhanced physical education is for children to engage in moderate to vigorous physical activity for at least 50 percent of class time. It is a challenging goal (e.g., Hollis et al., 2016), but it can be achieved by adjustments such as those described in the sections Carrying Out Enhanced Physical Education and Putting It Together: Practical Strategies for Your Physical Education Class.

What Principals, Teachers, and Parents Need to Know

Figure 5.2 summarizes the documented benefits of enhanced physical education. Share this information with principals, teachers, parents, and others.

Carrying Out Enhanced Physical Education

Two evidence-based curricula have been shown to increase children's moderate to vigorous physical activity during physical education classes:

- SPARK Program (Sports, Play, and Active Recreation for Kids) (Sallis et al., 1997; McKenzie et al., 2016)
- CATCH (Coordinated Approach to Child Health) (Luepker et al., 1996)

If resources allow, both curricula with accompanying professional development are available for purchase.

You can use a variety of teaching approaches to increase fundamental motor skills, including practice with a targeted skill focus and a game or physical activity focus (Tompsett et al., 2017; Barnett, 2016). Both

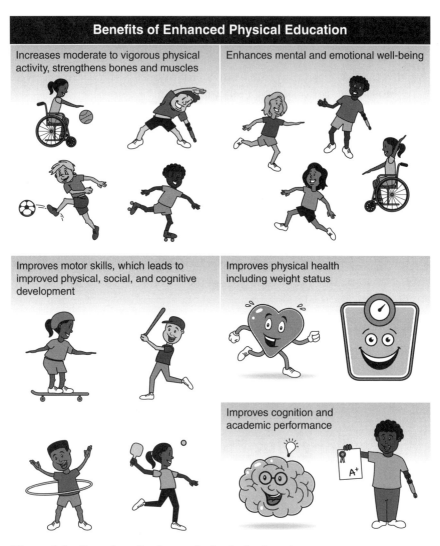

Figure 5.2 Benefits of enhanced physical education.

Information from HHS (2018); Hillman et al. (2019); Community Preventive Services Task Force (2013); Lonsdale et al. (2013); Hollis et al. (2016); Wong et al. (2021); García-Hermoso et al. (2020); Lorås (2020); Robinson et al. (2015).

From R.R. Pate and R.P. Saunders, *Promoting Elementary School Physical Activity: Ideas for Enjoyable Active Learning* (Champaign, IL: Human Kinetics, 2024).

approaches are more effective when carried out in an environment that supports student autonomy (Tompsett et al., 2017; Barnett et al., 2016). Creating a motivational climate that supports students' needs for autonomy, competence, and relatedness may entail a substantial change for many physical education teachers and may require professional development to fully carry out (Wong et al., 2021).

Several effective and practical approaches to increasing moderate to vigorous physical activity are available. These approaches focus on combinations of strategies that improve physical education class organization, management, and instruction; infuse higher-intensity physical activity; and enhance the motivational climate in physical education. Three practical models emphasize strategies to increase moderate to vigorous physical activity in physical education classes: LET US Play (Weaver et al., 2013), SAAFE (Lubans et al., 2017), and the SHARP Principles (Powell et al., 2016). All three programs have similarities. However, SAAFE and SHARP focus on fitness infusion and enhancing the motivational climate of students and teachers, respectively, to promote moderate to vigorous physical activity in physical education class.

LET US Play

The principles of LET US Play (Lines, Elimination, Team size, Uninvolved staff and kids, and Space, equipment, and rules) (Weaver et al., 2013) focus on these practical ways to increase moderate to vigorous physical activity in physical education:

- L = Reduce *lines* by providing more equipment.
- E = Get rid of *elimination* of physical activity in games (e.g., in games of tag, instead of freezing, children who are tagged can become additional taggers or perform an activity in place).
- T = Reduce the size of *teams* (use small-sided games, such as 3 vs. 3 rather than 10 vs. 10) and provide additional equipment. Large fields can also be divided into two or more smaller fields.
- U = Increase student and teacher involvement. Students may become *uninvolved* in large teams, long lines, or during elimination; smaller teams, eliminating lines, and removing elimination help. It is also important for the physical education teacher to become actively involved by moving through the space and encouraging children.
- S = Change the *space* (e.g., subdivide a large field), add more equipment of the right size and skill levels for the students, and change the rules (e.g., remove lines and elimination) to enhance physical activity.

Providing more equipment enables all children in physical education class to be physically active at the same time.

SAAFE

The teaching principles of SAAFE (Supportive, Active, Autonomous, Fair, and Enjoyable) (Lubans et al., 2017) address motivational climate as well as promote moderate to vigorous physical activity. SAAFE strategies are as follows:

- *Supportive:* Facilitate a supportive learning environment that cultivates feelings of autonomy, competence, and social cohesion. Supportive teachers are able to take the perspective of their students, provide explanations for what they are doing, use language that is not strict or controlling, and demonstrate emotional support. In contrast, a performance climate focuses on superior performance or winning.

- *Active:* Promote moderate to vigorous physical activity through having minimal lines, using small-sided games, avoiding elimination, integrating high-intensity bursts of physical activity, reducing transition time, and maximizing equipment.

- *Autonomous:* Provide students choices (2-4 opportunities within a session), involve them in creation and modification of activities and rules, and explain the reasoning for the different activities.

- *Fair:* Ensure all students have opportunities to experience success by minimizing competition, creating similar grouping of children for certain activities, modifying activities to level the playing field, and encouraging self-comparison (mastery) rather than peer comparison.
- *Enjoyable:* Design activities in which students can have choice, feel competent, and interact with others (social connection is important for enjoyment). Strategies to create enjoyment include providing variety in activities and equipment, starting and ending sessions with short activities that students like, and using appealing music.

SHARP

The SHARP principles (Powell et al., 2016) support teacher autonomy, competence, and relatedness to transform traditional physical education into enhanced physical education. The SHARP principles are as follows:

- S = Stretching while moving
  - Use dynamic movements and stretches to replace static ones during warm-ups.
  - Examples include side shuffles, jump and twist, high knees, heel flicks, jumping jacks, and skipping.
- H = High repetition of motor skills
  - Students become physically skilled by being engaged in physically active learning.
  - Examples include reducing or eliminating lines, having small-sided games or group work, and increasing the amount of equipment available to students.
- A = Accessibility through differentiation
  - Tasks for all children should be at a level appropriate to their physical, cognitive, and social development.
- R = Reducing sitting and standing
  - Teachers develop awareness of the amount of time students are sitting and standing as a first step toward reducing that time.
  - Strategies include providing targeted feedback to learners without stopping the whole class, engaging students in physical activity as early as possible in a session, and ensuring equipment is ready, organized, and accessible at the start of and throughout a session.
- P = Promoting in-class physical activity
  - Teachers verbally encourage students to be physically active and to participate throughout the session.

Putting It Together: Practical Strategies for Your Physical Education Class

This section incorporates principles and strategies from LET US Play, SAAFE, and SHARP into practical strategies you can use and adjust to fit your current practices in teaching physical education. The class period starts the moment students walk in and ends when they leave. Physical education should use a mastery (not performance) approach, include clear but brief explanations of activities, involve some student choice, have high levels of teacher engagement and involvement, and be fun and active.

A typical physical education class period may include the following:

- Student arrival
- Structured exercise or warm-up
- Skill demonstration and skill practice
- Game play
- Dismissal

Additional opportunities for physical activity during the physical education period include the following:

- Transitions
- Equipment distribution and collection

Enhanced physical education strives to increase the amount of physical activity during all parts of class, including the transitions between the parts, with the goal of keeping students involved in moderate to vigorous physical activity for at least 50 percent of class time. Following are some ideas that teachers have used successfully.

Student Arrival

Begin class with instant activity, such as the following:

- Walking or jogging around the space
- Playing a chase or tag game
- Playing music to set the stage for fun physical activity
- Posting the instant activity of the day for students to see when they arrive to class
- Having students immediately play a previously taught game or skill activity

While Taking Attendance

- Have students walk or jog the perimeter of the space. As they pass you, report each student's name.

- Designate student leaders during circuit stations to report attendance to you.
- Write students' names on popsicle sticks and spread them on the ground before class. As students arrive, they find and then place their stick in a collection box. Sticks not collected are counted as absent.

Structured Exercise or Warm-Up

- Structured exercise can be led by you, adult volunteers, or even students. The beginning routine can be new or one that is repeated daily.
- Emphasize moderate to vigorous physical activity by moving while stretching. For example, include dynamic movements and stretches, shuffles, jumps and twists, high knees, heel flicks, jumping jacks, and skips.
- Minimize the amount of time spent in verbal instruction; focus on moving. Here are some more suggestions for successfully leading structured exercise:
  - Use a previously taught exercise routine to music.
  - Allow students to suggest exercises or movements for the routine.
  - Use an exercise circuit (a rotation of strength-training exercises that work all parts of the body) with varying skills as a warm-up routine.

Skill Demonstration and Skill Practice

Encourage your students to be physically active while you are giving them instructions by doing the following:

- Keep instruction time brief.
- Ask students to stand instead of sit while they listen.
- Use active instruction, where students practice the skill as you teach.

Encourage your students to remain physically active as they learn new skills. During practice, try doing the following:

- Engage all students at the same time rather than individually while others wait in line.
- Give students enough time with equipment to master the skill. You may need to add extra equipment so that all students can be active.
- Place students into small groups (based on skill) practicing the same skill rather than one large group.

- Evaluate skill levels; teach more advanced skills as students achieve benchmarks.

Game Play

Give students clear, brief instructions and rationale.

- Consider creating multiple teams so that all students can participate in the game at the same time, or select a game that allows all students to participate (see Ideas for Enhanced Physical Education for ideas).
- Modify existing games to increase physical activity as follows:
  - Rotate positions during team sports so that all students have the opportunity to play all positions.
  - Reduce sedentary components of traditional games by having students play the games in smaller groups to have more access to equipment.
- Minimize the use of elimination in games.
  - Consider creative modifications to make these games more active and inclusive.
  - If you decide to play elimination games, give students who are eliminated an activity or exercise to do before rejoining the group rather than sitting out.

Transition and Waiting Times

Reduce or add movement to times when students are watching, listening, or waiting for instructions.

- Choose teams before starting the lesson. Use clothing, birthday month, or other student characteristics for random grouping, or have students find a partner by having every other person kneel or stand; kneelers and standers become different groups.
- To minimize lag time, use the same equipment for the warm-up as for the next part of the lesson.
- Ask students to walk or jog the perimeter, do jumping jacks, or do other movements while they are waiting.

Equipment Distribution and Collection

Try the following ideas to reduce down time at the beginning and end of physical education class:

- Set up equipment in the corners of the room or gym before class starts.

- Hand out equipment as students move around perimeter.
- Assign students to help distribute and collect equipment.
- Play a game that involves collecting equipment at the end of a game.

Physical Activity Ideas for Enhanced Physical Education

Fun, inclusive, and active games that you can adapt for your physical education class are summarized in table 5.1, and they are described in detail on the pages that follow.

Table 5.1 Sample Activities for Enhanced Physical Education

Name	Grades	Location
Aliens and Astronauts	4-5	Outdoors or gym
Hive	1-3	Outdoors or gym
Base Tag	K-5	Outdoors or gym
Borrow It	K-5	Outdoors or gym
Clothespin Tag	K-5	Outdoors or gym
Everybody Bats	K-5	Outdoors or gym
Everybody's It	K-5	Outdoors or gym
Ultimate Foam Ball	3-5	Outdoors or gym

ALIENS AND ASTRONAUTS

Type: Physical education

Target grades: 4-5

Equipment: None

Description: Participants form groups of four. Three group members hold hands, and the fourth member is outside the circle (the alien). One member in the circle is the captain of the spaceship; the other two are astronauts. The alien tries to capture the captain by running around the circle (not reaching through), while the astronauts try to protect the captain by moving around quickly while not releasing their hands. Have group members change roles often. Remind participants to keep their heads up and to be aware of others when moving through the space.

Variations: To decrease the challenge,

- have more astronauts in each group.
- require that aliens walk.
- allow aliens to use implements to help them tag captains (e.g., pool noodles).

To increase the challenge,

- decrease the number of astronauts.
- increase the number of aliens.

Adapted by permission from H. Gardner, *Physical Literacy on the Move. Games for Developing Confidence and Competence in Physical Activity* (Champaign, IL: Human Kinetics, 2017).

HIVE

Type: Physical education

Target grades: 1-3

Equipment: 8 to 10 hoops or mats

Description: Before beginning the activity, scatter 8 to 10 hoops or gymnasium mats around the activity space; they represent the beehives. Divide participants into groups of four or five. Groups travel together around the activity space as directed (e.g., walk, skip, hop, jog). When you call out "Honey time," each group moves to the beehive; and all participants try to fit into the hoop or onto the mat. Repeat the activity, each time removing one hoop or mat. More than one group can be on each hoop or mat, and groups should work together to include all members. Provide safe distances between hoops. Remind participants to keep their heads up and to be aware of others when moving through the space.

Variations: To decrease the challenge,

- use larger hoops or mats.
- create smaller groups.
- offer no time limit on the activity.

To increase the challenge,

- use smaller hoops or mats.

- provide a time limit for fitting into the hoop or onto the mat.

Adapted by permission from H. Gardner, *Physical Literacy on the Move. Games for Developing Confidence and Competence in Physical Activity* (Champaign, IL: Human Kinetics, 2017).

BASE TAG

Type: Physical education

Target grades: K-5

Equipment: A base (carpet square, poly spot, marker) for every three players and a foam ball for every five players

Description: Spread bases throughout the desired play area, with approximately one base for every three players. Have a player with a foam ball (an "It") for every five players. The "It" student throws the ball to try and hit another student, who tries to avoid being hit either by running out of the way or by getting safe on a base. If a non-It student is hit with a ball, that student becomes It and takes the ball to hit someone else who is not It. Students on a base are considered safe and cannot be It, even if they are hit. However, if one student is on a base and another student wants the occupied base, the student on the base must move off of it and cannot immediately return to the same base. The person wanting the base can say something to let the person on the base know that they must go, such as "Go" or "Bye-bye." Remind players to be alert and aware of each other to avoid crashes.

Variations:

- If you don't have any balls, then the Its simply tag the Not-Its.
- Use different sizes of balls to make the game more challenging.

Adapted by permission from D.N. Le Fevre, *Best New Games,* Updated Edition (Champaign, IL: Human Kinetics, 2012).

BORROW IT

Type: Physical education

Target grades: K-5

Equipment: Carpet squares or some other item, such as hoops, for bases, and enough objects (e.g., Frisbees, balls, stuffed animals) so that each team has four or five

Description: Divide the group into groups of four (another number works as long as all the groups are fairly close in number). Have each group choose four or five items (such as Frisbees, balls, stuffed animals) plus a base to put them on (or in; hoops work well). Have the groups spread out in a circle at least 10 feet (3 m) apart from one another; the ideal situation is to have all groups an equal distance from one another. After placing the items on their base or in their hoop, have all players put one foot on their base before starting.

When everyone is ready, count to three to start, after which every player will go to the bases of another group and borrow an object to bring back to their own base. A player can take no more than one object at a time, must place it (not throw it) on or in the base, and may not throw it to another player on their team. No player can guard their base or obstruct players from other teams; they can only get objects from other teams' bases. The game lasts only a minute, but it can go longer if your players have enough energy. The winner is the group who ends up with the most borrowed objects. Redistribute the objects and do it again, or move on to another game.

Variations: For younger players, you can set up groups shorter distances apart.

Adapted by permission from D.N. Le Fevre, *Best New Games*, Updated Edition (Champaign, IL: Human Kinetics, 2012).

CLOTHESPIN TAG

Type: Physical education

Target grades: K-5

Equipment: Clothespins (ideally three per student)

Description: Before starting, define the playing area. It should not be too big of a space, because students should be able to get to each other easily, but it should be large enough that everyone can move around comfortably. Distribute the clothespins and tell students to attach the pins on their shirt sleeves at shoulder level. If students do not have sleeves, they can put pins on the sides of their shirts at hip level. Students should not clip pins to their skin or to the front or back of their shirts, trousers, or skirts. If they do so, when others try to get the pins, it can get too personal, even if unintentionally.

At your signal, students move through the playing space and try to get as many clothespins from other students as possible. Each time a pin is obtained, the person getting it has three seconds to put it on their sleeve; they will count out loud "One, two, three." During this time, no one can take one of their pins; once they are finished, they are fair game once again. Players cannot guard their pins by putting their hands over them or by pushing other players' hands away.

Variations: Use flag football belts with the hook-and-loop flags rather than clothespins and allow more time, especially for younger children.

Adapted by permission from D.N. Le Fevre, *Best New Games,* Updated Edition (Champaign, IL: Human Kinetics, 2012).

EVERYBODY BATS

Type: Physical education

Target grades: K-5

Equipment: A bat, a large, soft ball such as a high-bounce foam ball, and a base

Description: Form two teams. Although ability level matters little, you can ask players to partner up with someone at about their own ability level and then have the partners split up to make the teams. The team batting sends up a batter; it does not matter who it is, because everyone will get a turn. The batter hits a ball gently pitched by someone from the opposing team. No matter where a struck ball goes—forward, sideways, or backward—the batter starts to run around their own team. Each circle around their team is a run, which the whole team counts out loud. The closer together teammates get, the shorter the distance the batter needs to run.

Meanwhile, it does not matter who has gotten the ball on the fielding team. The rest of the team will form a line behind that person, facing the same direction. The ball is passed back from teammate to teammate in the line, first between the legs and then the next one over the head; that pattern repeats until the ball reaches the end of the line. Then the last player in the line holds the ball in the air and shouts, "Done!"

The number of times the batter has circled the team while the fielded ball was being passed down the line is the number of runs they have made for the team. Every player on the batting team takes a turn, and the total runs of all of batters are added for the team's score. Then the opposing team has a similar turn at bat.

Variations: Using a large ball (even a beach ball) or a batting tee is especially important for younger players. The game can also be adapted for kickball.

Adapted by permission from D.N. Le Fevre, *Best New Games,* Updated Edition (Champaign, IL: Human Kinetics, 2012).

EVERYBODY'S IT

Type: Physical education

Target grades: K-5

Equipment: Boundary markers such as cones, poly spots, Frisbees, or other such indicators are useful. You can also use existing boundaries such as trees, sidewalks, and bushes.

Description: In this game of tag, everyone is It and can tag everyone else. Once a person gets tagged, they are frozen; when they are tagged again by anyone, they are unfrozen.

Variations: As with most active games, when players are moving about quickly, risk of collisions increases. To avoid crashes, remind players to be aware of where they are running. If that reminder doesn't work, try having them do a fast walk (one foot must be down before the other is up) or find another way of moving.

Adapted by permission from D.N. Le Fevre, *Best New Games,* Updated Edition (Champaign, IL: Human Kinetics, 2012).

ULTIMATE FOAM BALL

Type: Physical education

Target grades: 3-5

Equipment: A foam ball or another object that can be easily thrown, such as a foam disc or crumpled paper

Description: Establish a rectangular playing surface with two sidelines and end zones. Boundary markers are very helpful. The object for a team is to advance the foam ball so that it may be caught in its own end zone, which should be at least 10 feet (3 m) wide.

Divide the class into two teams. One team gets on the end of the playing surface that they are defending, then throws or kicks the ball to the other team on the opposite end of the playing surface. Either team's players can go anywhere on the playing surface, but they must keep at least an arm's length away from each other. The team with the object or ball cannot run with it; they must advance or move the ball only by passing it to a teammate. They lose possession of the ball if it touches the ground or is intercepted by the opposite team. Once a team scores, they return to the end of the playing surface they are defending and then repeat the start by kicking or throwing the object to the other team.

Tip: The advantage of playing with a foam ball is that nobody is an expert at throwing it. Avoid using a Frisbee because not everyone can throw it properly.

Variations: If players are too aggressive, make the distance the defense players must keep between themselves and offensive players two or more arm lengths.

Adapted by permission from D.N. Le Fevre, *Best New Games, Updated Edition* (Champaign, IL: Human Kinetics, 2012).

Summary

Enhanced physical education involves curricula and practice-based approaches to increase the amount of time students engage in moderate to vigorous physical activity during physical education classes. Effective strategies include improved class organization, management, and instruction; supplementing standard physical education classes with high-intensity activity; and incorporating motivational elements in teaching physical education. Engaging in moderate to vigorous physical activity is associated with numerous physical, mental, and cognitive benefits for children, and participating in enhanced physical education increases the percentage of time that students spend in moderate to vigorous physical activity. In addition, enhanced physical education has been shown to improve children's health-related physical fitness components, fundamental motor skills, and mental and emotional well-being. Physical education instructional time should total to a minimum of 150 minutes per week (30 minutes/day) in elementary schools. Students should spend at least 50 percent of class time in moderate to vigorous physical activity.

CHAPTER 6
PHYSICAL EDUCATION BEYOND THE GYMNASIUM

Quick Start

- *What?* In physical education beyond the gymnasium, the physical education teacher creates an enjoyable physical education environment with a positive motivational climate that results in students wanting to be physically active, connects students to physical activity opportunities during out-of-school time, and communicates with families about physical activity.

- *Why?* Participating in enjoyable physical activity during physical education makes students more inclined to participate in physical activity outside of physical education. Being linked to fun out-of-school opportunities for physical activity enables children to be physically active in school and community settings, which encourages lifelong physical activity.

- *Where, when, and who?* The physical education teacher creates a positive motivational climate for all students during physical education class and interacts with students in and out of class to encourage them to participate in specific out-of-school physical activity opportunities. The physical education teacher also communicates with parents and guardians and leaders of out-of-school physical activity opportunities as needed.

Details

This section provides background information on physical education beyond the gymnasium and discusses its benefits. It also includes information you can share with administrators, other teachers and school staff, and parents.

What Is Physical Education Beyond the Gymnasium?

An aim of physical education has long been to prepare students for a physically active lifestyle by developing their motor competence, physical activity knowledge, physical fitness, and personal and social responsibility (Webster et al., 2020; Pate et al., 2006). While it is important to address physical activity during physical education, it is also important to remember that physical education offers much more than simply providing physical activity during class (Webster et al., 2020). Physical education aims to develop students' skills, knowledge, and dispositions to participate in physical activity throughout life, and it provides meaningful experiences that enhance self-directed purpose to help achieve that goal (Webster et al., 2020). This chapter emphasizes some specific ways, beyond providing essential, standard physical education instruction, that enable physical education teachers to reach beyond the classroom.

In physical education beyond the gymnasium, the physical education teacher

1. creates an enjoyable and active physical education environment with a positive motivational climate that results in students wanting to be physically active beyond physical education;

2. encourages students to participate in specific physical activity opportunities during out-of-school time in both school and community settings; and

3. communicates with parents and guardians as well as leaders of school and community organizations and groups that provide out-of-school physical activity opportunities for children.

Figure 6.1 summarizes these elements, and the following sections discuss them further.

Creating a Positive Motivational Climate in Physical Education Class

Students are more likely to have an enjoyable experience in a physical education class that has a positive motivational environment. Enjoyment of physical activity in physical education makes students more inclined to participate in physical activity at other times. Chapter 5 discussed how physical education classrooms with motivational climates that strive to meet children's needs for autonomy, competence, and relatedness (Ryan & Deci, 2000; Niemiec & Ryan, 2009) enhance motivation and enjoyment in physical education (Sun et al., 2017; Vasconcellos et al., 2020) and promote increased moderate to vigorous physical activity during physical education (García-Hermoso, 2020; Lonsdale et al., 2013; Wong et al., 2021; Commu-

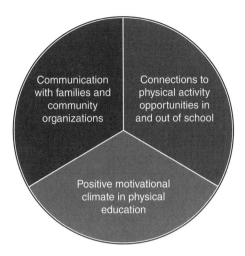

Figure 6.1   Elements of physical education beyond the gymnasium.

nity Preventive Services Task Force, 2014; HHS, 2018). This chapter focuses on how this positive motivational climate in physical education promotes physical activity engagement beyond the physical education setting. The student who finds physical education to be pleasurable and meaningful will be more motivated to participate in physical activity opportunities outside of physical education and in the future (Sun et al., 2017).

The features that create positive in-class motivational climates for students also result in physical education experiences that are relevant to students' lives. Elements of physical education teaching that help build meaning for students include encouraging positive social interactions, providing fun and enjoyable experiences, offering challenges at just-right levels of difficulty (not too easy and not too difficult), carefully considering use of competition, and developing motor competence (Beni et al., 2017; Ní Chróinín et al., 2018; Ennis, 2017).

Connecting Children to Out-of-School Physical Activity Opportunities

To promote physical activity, physical education needs to connect to the world outside the class. To create this link, the physical education teacher makes explicit connections between learning in physical education and life outside of physical education (Beni et al., 2017; Ní Chróinín et al., 2018; Ennis, 2017). For example, students need to know when, where, and how they can be physically active both in and outside the school setting (Cale & Harris, 2018). Children act on positive motivations to be physically active only if they know about and have access to fun physical activity opportunities.

The physical education teacher learns about students' physical activity interests as they encounter a variety of physical activities in physical education class and then encourages students to participate in out-of-school physical activity opportunities that align with those interests. This explicit connection enables students to act on positive motivations to participate in fun physical activity opportunities outside the school setting.

The physical education teacher identifies fun and accessible out-of-school physical activity opportunities available in the school and community through personal and professional networks. Out-of-school physical activity opportunities at the school may include programs for walking and biking to school; physical activity clubs and classes; voluntary, student-centered, and inclusive intramural programs; informal recreation or play on school grounds; integration of physical activity into homework during out-of-school hours; and, for higher grade levels, interscholastic sports (CDC, 2013).

Examples of physical activity opportunities in the community include organized youth sports, lessons (e.g., dance, yoga, martial arts), after-school programs that feature physical activity, physical activity clubs, summer camps, and sport camps. Local communities vary in the availability and accessibility of out-of-school physical activity opportunities. The physical education teacher can advocate for more school-based options if the community has limited opportunities or limited accessibility (see chapter 7).

Finally, the physical education teacher encourages students to participate in physical activity opportunities that have a good fit with their physical activity interests. Connecting students to physical activity opportunities can be as simple as providing verbal encouragement during student–teacher interactions. It can also be more involved, such as orchestrating communication with parents and community providers of physical activity opportunities, as discussed in the following section.

Communicating With the Gatekeepers of Child Physical Activity

Parents and guardians are important gatekeepers of their children's physical activity in the community. They can support their children's physical activity by modeling physical activity behavior, encouraging and watching their children participate in physical activities, and enabling them to be active in the community by facilitating program registration, obtaining needed equipment and clothing, and arranging transportation. Communities vary in access to safe physical activity space and opportunities. Therefore, to provide equitable, socially just, and inclusive experiences for children in physical education and to engage families, the physical education teacher needs to learn about children's family and community contexts (McMullen & Walton-Fisette, 2022).

Physical education teachers can communicate with families about what is happening in physical education and the importance of child physical activity outside of physical education (Egan & Miller, 2019). It is important for the physical education teacher to communicate with parents and guardians as well as with students about physical activity opportunities at the school or in the community. This way, students receive consistent messages from the physical education teacher and parents and guardians (Adams, 2019).

Parents and guardians are also instrumental in supporting child physical activity at home by purchasing physical activity equipment for home use, monitoring use of sedentary media, participating in physical activity with their children, encouraging their children to play out of doors, and allowing and encouraging their children to be active in the neighborhood (assuming it is a safe space). Simply spending time outdoors is associated with increased physical activity in children (Pate et al., 2019; Wilkie et al., 2018). Physical education teachers can provide information that will enable families to support children's physical activity at home and provide families with ideas about physical activities they can do with their children at home (Egan & Miller, 2019). Support to families for children's physical activity should be given with an understanding of the family and community context (McMullen & Walton-Fisette, 2022).

Other important gatekeepers for child physical activity are the leaders of organizations and groups that provide physical activity opportunities for children during out-of-school time. They can facilitate enrollment in physical activity programs, classes, clubs, and sports. They can also provide additional encouragement and support to students and families and work with the school to address accessibility and transportation for children.

Why Is This Important?

The U.S. Department of Health and Human Services (HHS, 2018b) issued physical activity guidelines to enable school-aged children and adolescents to achieve the health, social, emotional, cognitive, and academic benefits of regular physical activity. These guidelines recommend that children engage in at least 60 minutes of moderate to vigorous physical activity daily. Physical education can contribute toward this time, but it is rarely possible for children to get the full amount of recommended physical activity during physical education class. Most physical education classes are 30 minutes, and it is challenging for children to be moderately to vigorously active for even 15 minutes of that time (Hollis et al., 2016). To realize its benefits, it is imperative that physical activity take place outside of physical education and beyond the childhood years (Pate et al., 2006).

A child's experiences in physical education are foundational for physical activity that takes place outside of physical education as well as for physical activity in the future (Ladwig et al., 2018). Poor experiences in physical education are associated with negative feelings toward physical activity, lower intentions to be physically active, and sedentary behavior in adulthood (Ladwig et al., 2018). Extensive research on motivation in physical education shows that more self-determined motivation (which is supported in classrooms that address student needs for autonomy, competence, and relatedness) has many benefits, including student enjoyment, interest, effort, engagement, and intention to enroll in future physical education and to be physically active in the future (Sun et al., 2017).

Positive experiences in physical education create positive feelings, which are powerful influences on behavior. Classes with positive motivational climates that support children's needs for autonomy, competence, and belonging create internalized motivation for physical activity; in other words, children value and feel competent in physical activity, so they choose it.

Positive feelings and motivation for physical activity are translated to action when the physical education teacher encourages children to participate in specific opportunities that enable them to be physically active. Physical education teachers who observe and talk with their students, learn their physical activity likes and dislikes, and link them to opportunities outside physical education are simultaneously enhancing a positive social environment in class and promoting physical activity outside class.

When parents and guardians are also supportive of their children's physical activity at home, in the neighborhood, and in their community, children are more active. Parents play an important role in supporting their children's physical activity through encouragement, modeling physical activity, watching children being active, being active with their children, and providing transportation (Harrington et al., 2016; Gerards et al., 2021). Variation in community access to physical activity resources may be an issue for families, which makes school policies enabling community access to school facilities an important strategy for increasing physical activity options for children during out-of-school time. Children are more active if they receive encouragement from parents (Pate et al., 2019; Jaeschke, et al., 2017) and perceive more support from parents (Pate et al., 2019; Dowda et al., 2020).

Engaging community resources facilitates family access to community physical activity opportunities and enables the community organizations and groups to reach their audiences. Physical education teachers who develop working relationships and partnerships with leaders of community organizations that offer sports, physical activity lessons, and other opportunities may be better able to connect students to physical activity opportunities beyond the physical education class and for life (Pereira et al., 2021). As a bonus, community organizations and groups may be able to provide financial or in-kind resources to promote physical activity for children during the school day or during out-of-school hours (Egan & Miller, 2019; Adams, 2019) (see part III, The Physically Active School).

Increased physical activity and enjoyable experiences in out-of-school physical activity strengthen positive feelings and motivation for exercise. These feelings increase the likelihood of long-term physical activity, which in turn helps people achieve the many physical and mental health benefits of lifelong physical activity.

Carrying Out Physical Education Beyond the Gymnasium

Carrying out physical education beyond the gymnasium involves physical education teacher behaviors in three areas: creating the physical education classroom motivational climate, connecting children to opportunities in the school and community, and identifying and communicating with gatekeepers to children's out-of-school physical activity opportunities.

Creating a Positive Motivational Climate in Physical Education Class

Strategies for structuring a positive motivational climate in physical education class were presented in detail in chapter 5. Professional development will help teachers carry out these types of strategies. A summary of the key strategies to create positive motivational social climates in physical education class follows (Vasconcellos et al., 2020; Lubans et al., 2017).

To create an environment that builds student autonomy, as a physical education teacher you can do the following:

- Provide students with choices (two to four opportunities within a session).
- Involve students in the creation and modification of activities and rules.
- Explain the reasoning for the various activities.
- See each activity from the perspective of the students.
- Use language that is informational rather than strict or controlling.

To support children's need for competence or mastery, you can do the following:

- Minimize competition, performance, and winning; focus instead on participation, engagement, and effort.
- Create similar groupings of children for certain activities.
- Modify activities to level the playing field.
- Be patient and allow students to reach an understanding at their own pace.

© Human Kinetics

Fun physical activity in a supportive physical education environment creates motivated and engaged children.

- Encourage self-comparison (mastery) rather than peer comparison (competition).

To support children's need for relatedness, you can do the following:

- Show emotional support by listening to and accepting student expressions of negative feelings.
- Show enjoyment in interacting with students.
- Structure opportunities for students to interact with each other.
- Cultivate a sense of belonging and inclusion for all students.

Creating an environment that supports children's need to have choice, feel competent, and interact with others makes physical education an enjoyable experience. Other ways you can add to the fun in physical education are to offer a variety of physical activities and types of equipment and to play appealing music.

Connecting Children to Out-of-School Physical Activity Opportunities

Physical education teachers can identify potential opportunities in the school and local community based on personal and professional networks and connections and by searching for them. For older children, a homework assignment could be to identify and report on local physical activity resources as appropriate for the local community. Ideally, you identify a variety of opportunities that appeal to a wide range of children. These opportunities may include organized youth sports; swim, dance, yoga, or martial arts lessons; outdoor and adventure programs; after-school and aftercare programs that feature physical activity; physical activity and fitness clubs; and summer and sport camps. If communities lack physical activity resources, before- and after-school programs at school may be able to fill an important gap.

You can post physical activity opportunities on a bulletin board or website and keep it updated. You can approach students individually and encourage them to participate in physical activity opportunities that fit each student's interests and physical activity inclinations. You can also invite representatives from the various physical activity programs to visit and lead the class in a physically active demonstration to promote their program.

Communicating With the Gatekeepers of Children's Physical Activity

Four ways to engage families in promoting their child's physical activity are to

1. provide parents and guardians information about physical education, physical activity, and out-of-school opportunities;
2. design effective two-way communication with families;
3. assign physical activity homework that involves family members; and
4. have family events at school that include physical activity (Egan & Miller, 2019).

Many schools have a system in place to send or post information for parents and to enable two-way communication with parents. You may already use this system or may be able to build on it. Getting basic information to parents and guardians about the importance and benefits of physical education and physical activity is important. As a physical education teacher, it is essential that you establish two-way communication with parents and guardians. Effective communication with families will enable you to better understand the family and community context of students and to inform families about physical activity opportunities for their children in the school and community (Egan & Miller, 2019; Adams, 2019). Parents and guardians can be informed via social media, newsletters, or apps. You can assign family physical activity homework that involves physical activity logs, physical activity calendars, or physical activity bingo. You can also hold parent–teacher conferences, informational sessions (with physical activity), or active classes to increase parent and guardian knowledge of physical activity (Egan & Miller, 2019).

The first step in connecting with community groups and organizations that provide physical activity opportunities for children is to identify them. You may know about many of these opportunities through personal and professional networks, and you can use a process such as asset mapping to identify others (Egan & Miller, 2019). After identifying resources, you can make contact, communicate your interest in finding inclusive and enjoyable physical activity opportunities for students, learn about what the program offers, and find out how families can access the program.

Relationships with community organizations and groups are built over time. Connections with community groups and organizations can be informal, but you may wish to establish formal partnerships with community-based organizations, programs, or groups that can provide physical activity opportunities for children (Pereira et al., 2021; Egan & Miller, 2019; Adams, 2019). It may be possible to reduce barriers to access and to gain additional adult support for children's physical activity through these working relationships and partnerships.

Beyond sharing information, an effective way to engage both families and community organizations is to hold physical activity events at school, inviting families and community organizations to participate (Adams, 2019). Examples include family fitness nights, an annual fun run and walk, and family bowling nights (Adams, 2019). Such events will engage families, help recruit community partners to support school physical activity, and encourage students to be physically active during out-of-school time. Examples of community partners to invite and involve are the local bowling alley, tennis center, martial arts club, yoga studio, dance studio, and park and recreation center (Adams, 2019). Of course, planning and putting on these events can be time consuming. You may decide to make them part of a school-wide effort to promote physical activity that engages school resources including and beyond physical education (see part III, The Physically Active School).

Summary

Physical education emphasizes both behavior (being physically active) and instruction to develop motor competence, physical activity knowledge, physical fitness, and personal and social responsibility in order to prepare students for a physically active lifestyle (Webster et al., 2020). However, time and scheduling constraints inherent in the school day limit the amount of time in physical education, so children benefit from being connected to opportunities to be physically active outside of class. This chapter described three ways in which physical education teachers can facilitate student physical activity beyond the gymnasium and for life: having positive experiences during physical education, encouraging children to participate in school- and community-based physical activity opportunities, and reinforcing parents' efforts to support their children's physical activity.

THE PHYSICALLY ACTIVE SCHOOL

Part III is written for schools that are ready to coordinate a school-wide effort to maximize opportunities for students to be physically active and to enhance the school physical, policy, and social environments to create a physically active school.

Chapter 7 (Physical Activity Before and After School) describes how schools can provide physical activity opportunities during out-of-school time. It includes physical activity programs before and after school, and it demonstrates how schools can support walking and bicycling to and from school to increase students' physical activity time.

Chapter 8 (The Physically Active School Environment) explains how to strengthen the school physical activity environment to support a physically active school. It emphasizes the school's physical, policy, and social environments, including adult role modeling of physical activity.

Chapter 9 (Comprehensive School Physical Activity Program) defines the comprehensive school physical activity program and describes how to establish a strong foundation with the school physical activity committee and the school physical activity coordinator. It outlines the process for planning and conducting a comprehensive school physical activity program, which enables schools to put the ideas for physical activity opportunities presented in *IDEAL* into a coordinated, cohesive whole. In addition, it includes tips for monitoring and evaluating the program.

CHAPTER 7

PHYSICAL ACTIVITY BEFORE AND AFTER SCHOOL

Quick Start

- *What?* Before- and after-school physical activity programs provide supervised opportunities for children to be physically active immediately before and after school. Active transport is a planned process to provide children with safe walking and bicycling to and from school.

- *Why?* Both before- and after-school physical activity programs and active transport can increase the amount of activity that children get during the times immediately before and after school.

- *Who?* Before- and after-school physical activity programs and active transport to school should be available to all children regardless of income, color, gender, ability, or other differences. Ensuring effective and safe programs requires sustained collaborative efforts among school administrators and staff, students, parents, and community organizations.

- *Where and when?* Before- and after-school physical activity programs typically take place at school immediately before or after the school day. Active transport to and from school takes place before and after school on the route between the home and the school.

What Are Physical Activity Opportunities Before and After School?

Two types of physical activity opportunities take place before and after school: before- and after-school physical activity programs, and active transport to and from school.

107

Before- and After-School Physical Activity Programs

There is no set definition for before- and after-school programs, but they usually provide supervised physical activity at school, immediately before or after the school day (Demetriou et al., 2017). Examples include physical activity clubs such as running and walking clubs, supervised informal recreation or play, physical activity integrated into school-based childcare programs, and physical activity integrated into after-school programs (CDC, 2013). Programs may be delivered by school staff, community staff, or volunteers (CDC, 2013; Demetriou et al., 2017). Physical activity programs before or after school can also be provided by community organizations, such as the YMCA and local parks and recreation departments, and delivered in the school (CDC, 2013) or community settings (Demetriou et al., 2017). After-school programs are more common than before-school programs.

Active Transport

In contrast to motorized transportation, active transport is human-powered travel such as walking, bicycling, skateboarding, or riding a scooter. It has declined in the United States and around the world (Ikeda et al., 2020). In 2017, one in six parents in the United States reported that their youngest child walked to or from school (Omura et al., 2019). In 2017, 51.6 percent of elementary school students in the United States traveled to school by car, 36.4 percent by bus, 10 percent by walking, 0.9 percent by bicycling, and 1.1 percent by other modes (Kontou et al., 2020).

The primary barriers to active transport to school are living too far away from the school and concerns about traffic danger (Omura et al., 2019; Kontou et al., 2020). The median distance from home to school in 2017 was 2.1 miles (3.4 km) for elementary students in the United States. Walking trips to school are more common when the distance to school is one-half mile or less, and bicycling peaks between one-half and one mile. Active commuting to schools is lower in the South (8.7%) compared to the Northeast (20.8%), the Midwest (21.0%), and the West (21.2%) (Kontou et al., 2017). The schedule of the school day, especially early start times along with the complexities of family schedules, may also be a barrier.

Why Is This Important?

Before- and after-school programs and active transport to and from school provide chances for all students to be physically active before and after school. Additional benefits specific to these opportunities are discussed in this section.

Before- and After-School Programs

Providing physical activity opportunities before and after school for all students, including those with special needs; enables students to get more physically active time; be better prepared for learning; find out what activities they enjoy and may be able to do long term; and participate in safe, social, and supervised activities (CDC, 2013). The time before and after school is often sedentary, and before- and after-school physical activity opportunities especially benefit children who are the least active (Belton & O'Brien, 2020).

Studies have shown modest support for the effects of after-school programs on physical activity and body composition. Programs fared better when they were in school settings, provided sessions on two or more days per week, were offered for longer periods, and ensured high participation rates (Demetriou et al., 2017).

Fewer studies have been conducted on before-school physical activity programs. Little evidence exists for increased physical activity in these programs. However, suggestive support exists for fitness, readiness to learn, and academic performance (Woodforde et al., 2021).

Active Transport

Efforts to increase active travel to school are associated with increases in walking and bicycling to school, and active transport programs are considered promising for increasing child physical activity (Larouche et al., 2018; Community Preventive Services Task Force, 2018; Jones et al., 2019). Active transportation interventions in schools can also reduce risk for traffic-related injuries (Community Preventive Services Task Force, 2018). In addition, they have the potential to reduce air and noise pollution from motorized vehicles and reduce traffic congestion around the school (Smith et al., 2015; Buttazzoni et al., 2018; Jones et al., 2019).

Two examples of successful active transport approaches are the walking school bus (National Center for Safe Routes to School, n.d.) and Safe Routes to School (Safe Routes to School, n.d.a). Walking school bus programs are associated with more children walking to school based on self-report (Smith et al., 2015; Jones et al., 2019). Safe Routes to School programs are associated with increased walking and bicycling to school (McDonald et al., 2014) and reduced pedestrian and bicycling injuries (Community Preventive Services Task Force, 2018). Safe Routes to School programs that include both educational and infrastructure improvement strategies are more effective than those using a single strategy (Larouche et al., 2018).

Implementing Before- and After-School Physical Activity Programs

Before- and after-school physical activity programs are ideally tailored to a specific school with local planning. Consult the article "Seven Steps for Implementing Afterschool Programs: Strategies for Physical Educators" by Price-Shingles and Place (2016) for details and examples on how to plan and conduct an after-school program. A summary of this information is provided here:

- *Do a needs assessment.* This process includes getting input from students, school staff and administrators, parent–teacher organizations, booster clubs, and others using methods such as advisory groups, interviews, focus groups, and surveys. For a program to succeed, parents must be on board. Also, for safety, children need to be able to follow directions. To find potential partners and avoid duplication of efforts, identify local agencies such as libraries, cultural centers, and recreation centers near the school. For more ideas, review research and online resources, and learn about what other schools have done. You can benefit from others' experiences; no wheels need to be reinvented.

- *Design the program.* Use the information gathered in the first step to determine what kind of program and format will work for your school. Some options are drop-in formats where students can create their own activities, physical activity classes, and physical activity clubs.

- *Partner with community agencies.* Creating partnerships with local agencies can create additional resources for your program. Partners may include recreation centers, community centers, libraries, universities, and hospitals and clinics. Partners may be able to provide physical activity programming, which requires service contracts. They may be able to provide curricula or volunteer personnel, such as college students.

- *Identify available facilities.* Facilities, space, and equipment are often high-use areas after school. Gaining access may require diplomatic negotiation with existing clubs, sports teams, and other school and community events.

- *Obtain program funding.* Sustaining programming requires obtaining funding from public and private sources. Check the websites of public and private companies' community relations departments as well as federal and state funding sources. Consider having fees for program participation to help maintain it. However, you must also consider how to ensure that all students have equitable access.

- *Market the program.* Promote the program throughout the year, including through the summer months. Some ideas are to use existing school media outlets to promote the program; get on the agendas of meetings such as the school board, parent–teacher association, booster clubs, and others; and create and distribute flyers to send home with students.

- *Conduct an evaluation.* Collect information throughout the program to monitor student participation and attendance and to get feedback on the program activities. This information can be used to adjust the program as needed and to provide support for sustaining your program. Some methods for collecting information are surveys (such as a follow-up to the original needs assessment), roundtable discussions with student participants, interview or focus groups with parents of participating and nonparticipating students, and discussions or interviews with school staff involved in or affected by the program.

Of the few existing models of before-school physical activity programs, one successful example is Build Our Kids' Success (BOKS) for K-6 students (Cradock et al., 2019). Cradock and colleagues (2019) found that children participating in BOKS had higher levels of physical activity compared to children not participating. BOKS is offered at no cost, and it provides online resources and training for participating schools. The BOKS curriculum includes 12 weeks of physical activity instruction each semester, and it has sessions on nutrition. The program meets two or three days a week. BOKS may also be used during the school day and for physical activity breaks. To access the organization's resources, refer to its website.

Implementing Programs for Active Transport to School

A program for active transport to school is a joint school–community undertaking that involves collaboration among many organizations, ongoing communication and coordination, and an extensive planning process. Following are brief descriptions of walking school bus and Safe Routes to School programs. (For more detailed information on these programs, consult the websites in the reference list.) These two approaches can also be used together (Omura et al., 2019).

Walking School Bus

A walking school bus (Safe Routes, n.d.) can be informal, such as a small number of families taking turns to walk a group of children to school,

SDI/ E+/Getty Images Productions

An example of a walking school bus.

or it can be highly structured, involving specific routes, timetables, and trained volunteers (Smith et al., 2015). Formalizing the role of a paid walking school bus coordinator, who can also serve as a champion, is recommended (Smith et al., 2015). Distance between home and school is the most common barrier to active transport to and from school (Omura et al., 2019; Kontou et al., 2020). Schools have addressed this barrier by organizing stops within a mile of school where families and school buses can drop children off; adult escorts meet children and walk together the final distance to school (Omura et al., 2019).

Safe Routes to School

Safe Routes to School is a joint school–community project that is guided by these six principles (McDonald et al., 2014; Safe Routes to School, n.d.a.):

- *Education*: Providing students with the knowledge and skills for walking and bicycling safely
- *Encouragement*: Generating enthusiasm and excitement around walking or bicycling
- *Enforcement*: Ensuring safe driving behavior in school zones, often involving collaboration with law enforcement

- *Engineering:* Creating improvements in sidewalks, crosswalks, signage, and traffic calming near the school
- *Evaluation:* Assessing which approaches are working and identifying opportunities to improve the program
- *Equity:* Ensuring that the program is benefiting all, including low-income students, students of color, students of all genders, and students with disabilities

The following steps provide an overview of the planning process to conduct a Safe Routes to School program (Safe Routes to School, n.d.b.; Buttazzoni et al., 2018).

- *Bring together the right people.* The planning committee should consist of people from the school and community who are enthusiastic and committed to making walking and bicycling to school safe and attractive for all students. Group members can include school administrators, parents, students (including those with disabilities), parent organizations, teachers, staff, the school district transportation director, and adult school crossing guards. Community members can include neighborhood associations; local businesses; local pedestrian, bicycle, and safety advocates; and groups representing people with disabilities. Finally, include representatives from local government, including the mayor's office or council members, transportation or traffic engineers, local planners, public health professionals, and law enforcement. The committee can plan for a single school, a school district, or a larger region. The group will also need a coordinator.
- *Hold a kick-off meeting.* The purposes of this meeting are to create a vision, generate next steps, and form working committees. These committees may include mapping and information gathering, outreach, education and encouragement activities, enforcement and engineering, and traffic safety.
- *Gather information and identify issues.* It is important to understand the walking and bicycling conditions for students. For example, the planning committee can walk together around the school at arrival or dismissal time. Find out how many children currently walk or bicycle to school, and survey parents to find out their attitudes toward walking and bicycling. Identify issues that need to be addressed.
- *Identify solutions.* Solutions will be based on the Safe Routes to School framework and include a combination of education (e.g., pedestrian and bicycle safety for children), encouragement (e.g., special events titled Walk to School Day or Bike to School Day),

engineering (e.g., adding or improving sidewalks and crosswalks or paths), and enforcement strategies (e.g., working with law enforcement on unsafe driving in school zones and having trained crossing guards), while keeping equity for all children in mind. Select priorities among the issues and solutions generated in this and the previous steps.

- *Make a plan.* The plan should include encouragement, education, engineering, enforcement, and other strategies as well as a time schedule for each strategy, a map of the area covered by the plan, and a description of how the program will be evaluated.

- *Fund the plan.* Some parts of the plan (e.g., a kick-off event, walk to school day, new signs, fresh paint on the crosswalks) are low-cost projects. However, a project such as adding new sidewalks may take large amounts of funding. Places to search for funding include federal programs, state Safe Routes to School programs, environmental and air quality funds, health and physical activity funding sources, county and city funds, and philanthropic foundations.

- *Act on the plan.* Start with activities that do not require major funding to get some early wins. For children who live too far away from school to walk, one idea is to identify places were families can park away from school and walk the rest of the way to school. If traffic conditions are challenging, another idea is to start walking activities on the school grounds until improvements in the environment are made.

- *Evaluate, make improvements, and keep moving.* Monitor the numbers of participants and get feedback from students, families, and staff to find out what is working and what needs adjusting. Let people know about the successes. Look to the future by advocating for policy change, creating a permanent committee, and identifying additional champions.

Summary

Before-school physical activity programs, after-school physical activity programs, and programs for active travel to school can increase physical activity before and after school, when children are often sedentary. These approaches require coordinated efforts from administrators and staff, children and parents, school district representatives, and community agencies. In addition to having promise for contributing to children's total daily physical activity, these collaborative approaches can strengthen communities. The benefits for students, families, schools, and communities make the extra coordination effort worthwhile.

CHAPTER 8
THE PHYSICALLY ACTIVE SCHOOL ENVIRONMENT

Quick Start

- *What?* The four interacting parts of the physically active school environment are the physical environment, the social environment related to physical activity, physical activity policies, and physical activity practices.

- *Why?* The physical, social, policy, and program environments work together to encourage or discourage physical activity in the school setting. The policy environment conveys organizational commitment to physical activity, and it shapes decisions and actions about physical activity opportunities and the physical environment. The physical environment and physical activity program opportunities enable or constrain physical activity. The social environment related to physical activity encourages or discourages being physically active, and it conveys the school culture related to physical activity.

- *Where, who, and when?* The physically active school environment is ever present, and it applies to all spaces and aspects of the school. It affects all children and adults who spend time there.

What Is the Physically Active School Environment?

The physically active school environment provides easy ways for children and adults to participate in fun physical activity throughout the day. In the physically active school, physical activity is important to adults in the school and to children's families as well as to children who are students at the school. It is a supportive setting where physical activity feels natural. The physically active environment does not disrupt the academic focus of the school; instead, it contributes toward accomplishing its mission. This chapter describes the parts of the physically active school environment and how they can promote physical activity for everyone in the school. The physically active environment should accommodate children of all backgrounds, including those with diverse mental and physical abilities (McMullen & Walton-Fisette, 2022).

School environments, in which students spend much time, influence physical activity by enabling or constraining what is possible to do (Morton et al., 2016) and by providing cues about what is appropriate behavior in the school setting (Morton et al., 2016; Martin et al., 2014; Brittin et al., 2015). Environmental cues, which often affect behavior below conscious awareness, come from three interlinked aspects of the school setting: physical, social, and institutional environments (Morton et al., 2016; Martin et al., 2014; Brittin et al., 2015). The institutional environment includes physical activity policies and physical activity practices (see figure 8.1). Therefore, this chapter emphasizes four interacting components of the physically active school environment: physical environment, social environment related to physical activity, physical activity policies, and physical activity practices.

School Physical Environment

Features of the school physical environment related to physical activity include building design, types and configurations of furniture, amount and configuration of space indoors and outdoors, outdoor ground sur-

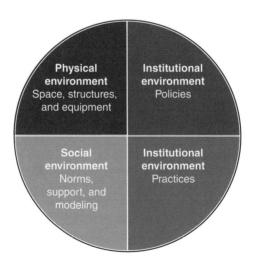

Figure 8.1 Components of the school environment that influence physical activity in children.

faces (e.g., paved, grass, natural surfaces), presence of facilities, and fixed and loose equipment inside and outside (Brittin et al., 2015; Morton et al., 2016). It includes having indoor space available for physical activity during inclement weather (Lounsbery et al., 2013).

School Social Environment

The social environment related to physical activity consists of social norms (the extent to which physical activity is encouraged or discouraged in that setting), expressions of social support or disapproval from peers and adults for participating in physical activity (Morton et al., 2016), and modeling of physical activity behavior (extent to which children and adults are seen being physically active) (Brittin et al., 2015). The motivational climate, which includes support of autonomy and relatedness as well as perception of mastery, is related to physical activity. How connected individuals feel to their school shows a promising positive association with physical activity (Morton et al., 2016).

School Physical Activity Policy Environment

The school institutional environment includes policies and in-school rules (Morton et al., 2016). Policies are written, formal, and often presented in official school policy and procedure manuals or employee handbooks (Lounsbery, 2017; Lounsbery et al., 2019). Policies seek to change systems to create supportive programs and environments (Woods et al., 2021). School physical activity policies inform school decisions and actions (practices) related to availability of physical activity facilities and physical activity programming (opportunities) in schools (Lounsbery, 2017; Lounsbery et al., 2019). As such, they affect whether physical activity opportunities are provided and accessible to all students, and they affect the quality of these opportunities. For example, school policies or rules can prohibit withholding recess and using physical activity as punishment and ensure that facilities are accessible to all students (Lounsbery et al., 2013; CDC, 2017).

Except for physical education, few formal physical activity policies exist in schools in the United States (Lounsbery et al., 2019) and most of them are at the district rather than school level (Lounsbery, 2017; Lounsbery et al., 2019). Most school policy studies report a combination of policies and school practices.

School Physical Activity Practices Environment

The school institutional environment also includes school decisions and actions, which are known as school physical activity practices (Lounsbery,

2017; Lounsbery et al., 2019). Practices are what schools do—the frequency and duration of programs (e.g., physical education, recess, classroom physical activity breaks, and other physical activity opportunities described in *IDEAL*), how and by whom programs are delivered, and the extent to which program leaders are provided training (Lounsbery, 2017; Lounsbery et al., 2019).

Why Is This Important?

This section provides information about the different aspects of the school environment and their importance for learning, physical activity, and social development.

School Physical Environment

The importance of the classroom space and configuration for promoting learning and physical activity was presented in chapter 4. This chapter focuses on the physical environment of the whole school—indoors and outdoors. Features of the school physical environment are clearly related to physical activity in children, especially when accompanied by adult supervision (Brittin et al., 2015). These features include the following:

- Multiple and varied outdoor fitness facilities (e.g., basketball hoops, soccer goal, running and walking track, ball field) that are appropriate for grade levels of children
- Indoor gymnasium
- Indoor and outdoor facilities to accommodate the use of fixed and moveable equipment
- Both hard and soft surfaces, as well as green or natural areas on the school grounds
- Variations in sun and shade in outdoor play and physical activity areas
- Age-appropriate fixed equipment on the playground
- Less-structured space with portable equipment on the playground, including field space
- Signage with point of decision prompts for stair use and other physical activity opportunities
- Multicolor ground marks in playground areas to delineate spaces for many types of activities

Research also shows that simply being outdoors increases physical activity in children (Gray et al., 2015; Brittin et al., 2015; Pate et al., 2019). This correlation is an important reason for children to spend time out of doors at school and to have recess.

School Social Environment

The importance of a positive motivational climate and for teachers to encourage physical activity in both the classroom and in physical education was presented in chapters 4 and 5. The motivational climate of the school beyond physical education is also important, and evidence shows the association between school connectedness and physical activity (Morton et al., 2016). School connectedness, the belief held by students that adults and peers in the school care about their learning as well as about them as individuals (CDC, 2009), has many academic, health, and developmental benefits for children (CDC, 2009; London et al., 2015). High-quality recess may contribute to a positive school climate that includes school connectedness, especially in low-income elementary schools (London et al., 2015). Interventions that involve outdoor play, social interactions, and contact with nature can improve both physical activity and school connectedness (Wray et al., 2020).

Staff involvement, one of the elements of a comprehensive school physical activity program, contributes to a positive school culture for physical activity. Staff can be involved in these four ways (CDC, 2013):

- Providing physical activity opportunities through classroom physical activity breaks, physically active instruction, recess, and other school physical activity opportunities
- Encouraging student participation in school physical activity opportunities
- Serving as positive physical activity role models in and out of school
- Participating in staff wellness programs that provide physical activity at school

Staff wellness programs that provide physical activity opportunities for adults at school directly improve staff health and increase physical activity levels. Adult physical activity can influence child physical activity; it shows that physical activity is accepted school behavior, helps build a physically active school culture, and creates motivated adults who provide more physical activity, encouragement, and support to children (CDC, 2013; Walker et al., 2021).

School Policy Environment

Formal physical activity policies are desirable because they reflect organizational commitment to physical activity and are sustainable (Lounsbery et al., 2019; Fair et al., 2018). Strong support exists for mandated minimum physical education time, requiring professional licensure of physical education teachers, adhering to physical education standards, and regular evaluation of physical education outcomes (Woods et al.,

2021; Gelius et al., 2020). In primary school settings, support exists for providing before- and after-school physical activity opportunities, free-play activities (especially for pre-K and K), integration of physical activity into classroom time, and opening school facilities to local communities through shared use agreements (Woods et al., 2021; Gelius et al., 2020). Promising evidence exists for active transport policy, although the local environment affects how well policies can be enacted at a school (Woods et al., 2021).

School Practices Environment

Evidence supporting the benefits of providing multiple opportunities for fun physical activity before, during, and after the school day has been discussed in previous chapters; here is a summary:

- Physical education, which is institutionalized in most U.S. schools, provides physical activity for students during the school day, links children to physical activity opportunities outside of physical education and school, and promotes lifelong physical activity (chapters 5 and 6).
- Classroom teachers provide physical activity opportunities during the school day with physical activity breaks and physically active instruction (chapters 1 and 2).
- Classroom teachers provide classroom environments that promote physical activity (chapter 4).
- Recess has long been a part of the elementary school day, and enhanced recess provides more opportunities for children to be physically active (chapter 3).
- Before- and after-school physical activity opportunities include free play and organized physical activity before and after school as well as active travel to and from school (chapter 7).

Having multiple opportunities for fun physical activity throughout the school day enables children to participate in the moderate to vigorous physical activity needed to gain health, social, and academic benefits. It also contributes toward a physically active school culture.

Interplay Between the School Physical, Social, Policy, and Practice Environments

The physical, social, policy, and practice environments work together to encourage or discourage physical activity in the school setting. Physical activity opportunities may not have a positive impact on academic outcomes and physical activity if the social environment is not supportive or if it emphasizes performance rather than mastery. A positive motivational climate and great physical activity spaces are much less effective without opportunities for fun physical activity.

Elements of the physical environment, such as the presence of spaces, facilities, and equipment that are accessible to all children, shape supportive social norms for physical activity at school. The presence of active children and adults in a variety of physical activity opportunities at school conveys a physically active school climate. Supportive physical activity policies show administrative backing for a physically active school. Together, physical, social, policy, and program environments reinforce each other to create the physically active school.

Carrying Out the Physically Active School Environment

Creating and enhancing the physically active school environment can be accomplished as part of planning and conducting a comprehensive school physical activity program. This process is presented in chapter 9, which describes the tasks involved in forming a school physical activity committee and hiring or appointing a school physical activity coordinator. Together the coordinator and committee guide the process of assessing the school environment and physical activity opportunities, developing a plan for action based on these results, and carrying out the plan to create a physically active school. The following sections focus on additional considerations that are important for effecting school physical environment, social environment, and policy change.

School Physical Environment

Beyond reconfigurations of classroom furniture and space, changing the school environment may seem daunting. Improving or adding fixed environmental features can require substantial resources, as well as causing disruption from construction. Changing, adding, or removing physical activity facilities, such as fixed playground equipment or markings, may raise safety concerns or require policy change (see the next section on enhancing the school policy environment). It is important to have some open space for play and physical activity. Changes such as obtaining additional portable equipment for use in classes and at recess may be easier to make. These changes may require fewer resources to obtain, or they may be donated by a community partner.

For schools with limited resources, a good approach is to be creative and work within the existing school environment, at least in the short run. Parent–teacher organizations can help with fundraising. If it is not feasible to change the school physical environment, change your attitude; focus on resources that are available and what you can do with them (Acosta et al., 2021).

School Social Environment

A school social environment that promotes physical activity has a positive motivational climate, facilitates school connectedness through physical activity opportunities such as quality recess, and has school staff providing physical activity opportunities at school, encouraging children to be physically active, and participating in physical activity at school. You can review these concepts in previous chapters as follows:

- How to facilitate positive motivational climates for students was presented in chapters 4 and 5.
- Strategies for providing high-quality recess were presented in chapter 3.
- Teacher roles in providing opportunities for physical activity were covered in chapters 1, 2, and 7.

In addition, review the online resource for creating school connectedness (CDC, n.d.).

This section focuses on staff physical activity modeling through school-based wellness programs. A staff wellness program that features physical activity opportunities for adults in the school can be part of the school's comprehensive school physical activity program (see chapter 9). The following is an overview of the steps to providing a walking program for adults in the school based on experiences of one elementary school (Langley & Lulinna, 2018).

- *Gain support and approval.* Administrative support at the school and district levels is essential to starting and maintaining the program. Talk to school staff; find out how a walking program could meet their needs. Talk about the benefits of walking. If you learn they would prefer a different program, provide the physical activity program that they want. The staff wellness program should meet the needs of staff. It is also important to communicate with parents, students, and community members.
- *Lay out a walking path on campus.* If a path or track does not exist, work with the appropriate people in the school to map out a route that can be used for the walking program. Measure the distance and mark the path, or create simple maps.
- *Set scheduled times for walking (if you would like to coordinate a student and staff walking program) or allow staff members to walk at any time during the workday that suits their schedule.* School policy or practice change may be needed to enable staff to walk at school during the

workday. It is fine to walk several times a day for short durations (such as 10 minutes).

- *Devise methods for individuals to track their walking.* Pedometers, phone apps, or other technologies are available to most adults, or a community partner may be able to donate them. If technology is not available, adults can count and record laps. Alternatively, develop a centralized method of monitoring walking; this approach requires staff or volunteers and works best with a set schedule for walking.

- *Promote your walking program.* Use existing communication strategies available at your school to advertise your program, including the morning broadcast, staff meetings, website, social media, and email.

- *Keep it fun and interesting.* Here are some ideas:
  - Encourage participants to find a walking buddy.
  - Encourage participants to set personal goals to walk a certain distance. Teams could keep track of distances and set a goal to "walk across the state" or to another destination.
  - Introduce seasonal walking events.
  - Sponsor friendly group walking challenges.
  - Ask participants what would keep them going.

An alternative to providing physical activity opportunities for adults during the school day is for the school or school district to partner with

© Human Kinetics

Teachers enjoy a wellness walk together.

a local gym or wellness provider to offer discounted memberships, programs, or classes for teachers at times that work in their schedule.

A comprehensive resource for planning and carrying out staff wellness programs, "Healthy School, Healthy Staff, Healthy Students. A Guide to Improving School Employee Wellness," is available through the Centers for Disease Control and Prevention (NACDD, 2018).

School Policy Environment

The process of implementing school policies is complex and not well understood (Lounsbery, 2017). The level of the policy is important (Lounsbery, 2017). School policies in the United States operate at the federal, state, school district, school, and class levels. Each level has a different policy-making body or policy maker. For example, the state level has a governor, legislature, superintendent of education, board of education, and department of education. Enacting change in state laws generally requires a coordinated advocacy campaign from a state-level coalition of dedicated people working together over years, which is beyond the scope of this book. Nonetheless, state laws pertaining to physical education in the United States do exist. A review reveals that stronger physical education laws, mostly related to the frequency and duration of physical education class, result in more physical activity among youth, and that state physical education laws are effective to the extent local school districts and schools implement them (An et al., 2021). It is important that school staff and parents be aware of the physical education and physical activity laws in place in their state.

Most schools interested in promoting physical activity will operate at the level of school district, school, and class, although schools strive to remain compliant with relevant federal and state laws and policies. Different strategies are needed to facilitate change at each of these levels, and formal policies are often at the school district level. At the school and class levels are often school regulations, rules, and less formal school practices related to physical activity (Lounsbery, 2017).

The content of physical activity policies affects the school physical activity environment and the provision of physical activity opportunities before, during, and after the school day. Language for effective policies is clear and specific; for example, wording such as "should" or "is encouraged" is less effective than "must" and "is required" (Lounsbery, 2017). Implementing policies can be a challenge for schools because of limited school resources, lack of procedures to install policy, and lack of accountability for noncompliance (Lounsbery, 2017).

The process for change in school policies and practices is advocacy. In this process, a dedicated individual, such as a physical education teacher, school physical activity coordinator, or parent, or a group, such as the school physical activity committee (see chapter 9), promotes a specific cause. Communication is directed toward the policy-making body or policy maker as well as others who might want to join the cause. Lounsbery (2017) describes advocacy as working to change the following:

- *Knowledge,* by bringing awareness to current practice and its problems
- *Values perspective,* by creating personal, social, and financial investment in the cause
- *Policy,* by promoting policy development, adoption, and change

Depending on the level of change needed, policy decision bodies and policy makers may be at the district level (e.g., school board, superintendent, curriculum director) or the school level (e.g., principal, curriculum coordinator), and some physical activity practice changes take place at the classroom level (Lounsbery, 2017). Table 8.1 outlines possible policy areas with examples of specific policies at the school level to support physical activity in elementary schools.

Table 8.1   Sample Policy Areas and Specific Policies for Elementary Schools

Policy area	School-level policy
Physical activity opportunities or programs	School has a comprehensive school physical activity program. Physical education provides 150 minutes of instructional time weekly. Physical activity is provided during the school day in classrooms. Recess is provided 20 minutes or more daily. Active transport to and from school is supported. Students are engaged in moderate to vigorous physical activity for 50 percent of physical education class time.
Training for staff delivering physical activity opportunities	Physical education teachers receive annual professional development. Adults providing physical activity opportunities are provided training.
Student access to physical activity opportunities at school	Physical activity cannot be administered for punishment. Physical activity opportunities, including recess, cannot be withheld for punishment. Indoor space is available for physical education and recess in bad weather.

(continued)

Table 8.1   *(continued)*

Policy area	School-level policy
Engaged families and community members and agencies	Families can serve as physical activity volunteers at school. School and community physical activity partnerships are supported.
Leadership and accountability	School has someone to oversee or coordinate a comprehensive school physical activity program.

Adapted from Lounsbery et al. (2019); CDC (2016); National Physical Activity Plan, Education Sector; National Association of State Boards of Education, State Policy Database.

Summary

The physically active school environment makes it easy for children and adults to participate in fun physical activity throughout the school day. It creates a supportive physical activity culture and enables people to be physically active by making the best use of physical environment resources, enhancing the social environment to encourage physical activity, enacting supportive school physical activity policies, and providing fun, accessible physical activity opportunities for students and adults.

CHAPTER 9
COMPREHENSIVE SCHOOL PHYSICAL ACTIVITY PROGRAM

Quick Start

- *What?* A comprehensive school physical activity program has five components to provide students with physical activity opportunities at school: physical education, physical activity during school (recess, classroom physical activity breaks, physically active instruction), physical activity before and after school (including walking and bicycling to and from school), staff involvement (staff wellness), and family and community engagement.

- *Why?* Comprehensive school physical activity programs provide a coordinated approach to offering a variety of daily physical activity opportunities in a supportive school environment. Multicomponent comprehensive school physical activity programs have positive effects on physical activity levels, fitness, motor skills, and sedentariness. They prepare students for a lifetime of physical activity, and they promote students' physical, social, and academic development.

- *Where and when?* Comprehensive school physical activity program activities take place at school before, during, and after the school day.

- *Who?* The comprehensive school physical activity program is coordinated and managed by an appointed or hired school physical activity coordinator along with a school physical activity committee that has diverse membership. The program provides physical activity opportunities for all children regardless of income, race, ethnicity, sex, gender identity, sexual identity, religion, physical or mental ability, appearance, or other characteristics (McMullen & Walton-Fisette, 2022).

- *How much?* Comprehensive school physical activity programs with multiple components enable children to accumulate 60 minutes of moderate to vigorous physical activity daily.

What Is a Comprehensive School Physical Activity Program?

A comprehensive school physical activity program is a school-level effort that requires ongoing, tangible support from school leadership as well as widespread participation from school staff, teachers, parents, and students. The program is designed to provide and coordinate a variety of opportunities for fun physical activity for all students in an environment that supports physical activity. It maximizes the number of physical activity opportunities for students before, during, and after the school day, and it organizes and puts into practice all the *IDEAL* ideas for promoting physical activity in your elementary school.

Here are the goals of a comprehensive school physical activity program:

- Provide a variety of physical activity opportunities that enable students to participate in a total of 60 minutes of moderate to vigorous physical activity per day (Webster et al., 2020; CDC, 2013; Pate et al., 2006).

Mark Bowden/Getty Images/iStockphoto

Comprehensive school physical activity programs enable all children to experience the health, social, and academic benefits of physical activity.

- Prepare students for a lifetime of physical activity (Webster et al., 2020; CDC, 2013; Pate et al., 2006).
- Promote comprehensive student development (physical, social, and academic) (Webster et al., 2020).

Who Makes the Comprehensive School Physical Activity Program Work?

The comprehensive school physical activity program is coordinated by an appointed or hired school physical activity coordinator along with a school physical activity committee that has diverse membership (CDC, 2013).

School Physical Activity Coordinator

The school physical activity coordinator (also known as the physical activity leader) is the driver for promoting physical activity in the whole school. This person manages all components of the coordinated school physical activity program, which potentially includes enhanced physical education; physical activity during the day including recess, physically active instruction, and physical activity breaks; school staff involvement including employee wellness; physical activity before and after school including physically active transport (walking and bicycling to school); and family and community engagement.

The school physical activity coordinator does not directly do all of these things; instead, this person works with the school physical activity committee to identify people in the school and community who carry out each school-based physical activity opportunity. The coordinator and committee also facilitate professional development for school personnel and provision of ongoing support to them as they carry out their tasks.

The physical education teacher is often identified as the most qualified person in the school to take on the role of school physical activity coordinator (CDC, 2013). However, the physical education teacher already has a full-time job, and even an enthusiastic physical education teacher may not find it feasible to take on the additional responsibility (Carson et al., 2020; Webster et al., 2020). One alternative is to hire a school physical activity coordinator who serves in that role only, although doing so requires an investment of additional resources (Brusseau & Burns, 2020). Another option is for a small team (no more than three people) to co-coordinate; each person would be responsible for different aspects of the comprehensive school physical activity program (Hivner et al., 2019).

Effective School Physical Activity Coordinators are invested in serving in that role (Carson et al., 2020) and receive additional professional development and technical assistance to carry it out (CDC, 2013; Webster et al., 2015; Brusseau & Burns, 2020). Online resources are available through the Centers for Disease Control and Prevention (CDC) and SHAPE America.

School Physical Activity Committee

The school physical activity committee, with the leadership and facilitation from the school physical activity coordinator, oversees the comprehensive school physical activity program. This group can identify, manage, and in some cases, provide resources for school physical activity.

Ideally, this committee will be a subcommittee of an existing school committee, such as the school health council or the school wellness committee. The committee should have diverse membership to include people from the school and community who have interest and experience with student education and health. Potential members include health and physical education teachers, other teachers, school staff such as the school nurse and media specialist, parent organizations and parents, students, school and district administrators, school board representatives, community health department representatives, college and university teaching and research faculty members, community agency leaders, community members, and local businesses. Most committees will have a subset of these possible members. All members of the group should be committed to children's academic success, health, and well-being, and they should know the school and community. Each member of the committee brings something of value to the group.

- *The school principal, administrators, and school board members* can provide essential support and access to resources as well as lend legitimacy to the group.
- *People from the health department, community agencies, universities and colleges, and businesses* can bring in-kind or financial resources to promote physical activity in the school and expertise in managing resources and program planning, implementing, and evaluation.
- *Physical education and classroom teachers and school staff* bring the most direct knowledge of the students. They can serve as the implementers for the physical activity opportunities and new school policies and practices to support physical activity.
- *Parent groups and parents* can help raise funds, voice support for physical activity to school and district decision makers, encourage child participation in physical activity, and potentially serve as volunteers for physical activity opportunities before, during, or after school.

What Are the Components of a Comprehensive School Physical Activity Program?

A comprehensive school physical activity program has five coordinated parts (see table 9.1), each of which has been discussed in previous chapters in *IDEAL* (CDC, 2013):

- Enhanced physical education
- Physical activity during the school day, including recess, physical activity integrated into instruction, and physical activity breaks in and outside the classroom
- Physical activity before and after school
- Staff involvement, including school employee wellness
- Family and community engagement

Table 9.1   The Five-Component Comprehensive School Physical Activity Program and *IDEAL*

Component	Physical activity opportunities	Chapter in *IDEAL*
Physical education	Enhanced physical education	5 and 6
Physical activity during the school day	Classroom physical activity breaks	1
	Physically active instruction	2
	Recess and enhanced recess	3
	Physically active classroom	4
Physical activity before and after school	Before- and after-school physical activity programs	7
	Active transport to and from school	7
Staff involvement	Staff wellness participation	8
	Teachers and staff providing physical activity opportunities	1, 2, 3, 4, 5, 6, and 7
Family and community engagement	Families being engaged	6 and 9
	Community organizations being engaged	8 and 9

How Much Is Enough?

As presented throughout *IDEAL*, higher levels of physical activity are linked to better health, social, emotional, cognitive, and academic outcomes in children. Nevertheless, children in the United States are not sufficiently active to achieve these benefits (HHS, 2018). For children to meet these guidelines and achieve the many benefits of regular physical activity, they must have fun, easily accessible opportunities to be physically active. This is where the comprehensive school physical activity program comes in.

Children spend most of their time in school. Because of time and scheduling constraints, no single physical activity opportunity at school—even if it's of the highest quality—provides 60 minutes of moderate to vigorous physical activity. For example, it is challenging for a 30-minute physical education class to yield 15 minutes of moderate to vigorous physical activity toward the 60-minute goal. However, if multiple additional opportunities exist in the classroom, recess, and after school and those opportunities reach all students, the time adds up.

Does every school need to implement all components of a comprehensive school physical activity program to achieve the academic and health benefits for children? Too few studies have looked at this question to know an answer yet. It may be best for schools to think of the five-part comprehensive school physical activity model as a guide for planning. For example, some schools may be able to achieve the goals of a comprehensive school physical activity program with fewer than five components (Webster et al., 2020). Even if a school strives toward five components, it may be wise to phase in the parts over time, learning and gaining experience with each addition (CDC, 2013; Hivner et al., 2019).

Why Is This Important?

A comprehensive school physical activity program is an example of a multicomponent physical activity program. A review of multicomponent school-based physical activity programs showed that most feature physical education plus one or two additional components—usually physical activity during the school day, such as classroom physical activity. Staff involvement (including wellness programs for adults) and family and community engagement were the least common components (Pulling Kuhn et al., 2021).

Multicomponent physical activity intervention studies found positive effects on physical activity levels, fitness, motor skills, and sedentariness; few looked at cognitive or academic benefits (Pulling Kuhn et al., 2021). Earlier reviews (Chen & Gu, 2018; Erwin et al., 2013) and a review of reviews across settings (Messing et al., 2019) found similar, positive results.

They also showed limited inclusion of staff wellness program and family and community engagement, even though these elements show promise for enhancing children's physical activity.

Support exists for the effectiveness of individual components of a comprehensive school physical activity program to increase physical activity and improve classroom behavior and academic performance when considered separately, as presented in earlier chapters. However, few schools have carried out the full five-component school physical activity program, which limits what is known about the effects of the full five-component model (Chen & Gu, 2018; Erwin et al., 2013). It is promising that effectiveness for increasing physical activity increases as more components are included (Brusseau & Burns, 2020). Other promising effects of multicomponent school physical activity programs include improving children's physical activity enjoyment, classroom on-task behavior, and metabolic health (Brusseau & Burns, 2020).

What Is Involved in Planning and Conducting a Comprehensive School Physical Activity Program?

The CDC created a guide for planning, conducting, and evaluating a comprehensive school physical activity program called Comprehensive School Physical Activity Programs: A Guide for Schools (CDC, 2013). The CDC guide provides details on how to prepare for, carry out, and evaluate a comprehensive school physical activity program and includes helpful templates and checklists to aid the planning process. The organization also provides a compilation of resources to assist schools with comprehensive school physical activity programs in Increasing Physical Education and Physical Activity: A Framework for Schools (CDC, 2019). It is recommended that you consult these guidelines as you plan your program. Hivner & colleagues (2019) present a useful application of the CDC guidelines in "When a 'One Size' Model Doesn't Fit All: The Building Healthy Schools Program." The material summarized next is based on the CDC (2013) materials.

The steps involved in planning and conducting an effective comprehensive school physical activity program are a series of nonlinear tasks; an earlier step may be revisited several times and at any point in the process (see figure 9.1).

- Create and grow the foundation for the comprehensive school physical activity program by forming a school physical activity committee and hiring or appointing an individual to serve in the role of school physical activity coordinator.

- Take stock of existing physical activity opportunities and the school physical activity environment as well as school resources and challenges in these areas and create a vision for your comprehensive school physical activity program.
- Select priorities for action (providing physical activity opportunities and enhancing the physical activity environment).
- Plan the details (who does what, when, where, and how; i.e., the resources needed).
- Provide professional development and training and plan ongoing support. Free resources are available online through the CDC and SHAPE America, and community partners may be able to provide additional resources including training.
- Promote the comprehensive school physical activity program and physical activity opportunities.
- Carry out the plan and keep track of the opportunities for physical activity offered, how many students participate, and the way students and staff react to them.
- Learn from experience to grow the physically active school.

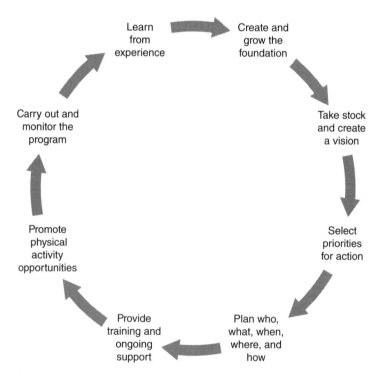

Figure 9.1   Planning and conducting a comprehensive physical activity program.

Learning From Experience

To keep your comprehensive school physical activity program on track, document and monitor what is happening as it is happening. Informally, you can talk to students, teachers, school staff, parents, and others involved in the program to find out what physical activity opportunities were provided, how many children attended, and how children and adults reacted to the physical activity opportunities. More formally, you can collect information using attendance sheets, short surveys, interviews, and focus groups or roundtables.

Documenting program activities and getting feedback from participants and staff is appropriate for a one- to two-year-old comprehensive school physical activity program. Indeed, it may be the only evaluation approach some schools ever choose to take. However, after the program is well established, the school physical activity committee and coordinator may want to know about the effects of the program on student behavior or academic outcomes. A useful approach for conducting more advanced program evaluation is to find an evaluation expert with whom you can collaborate. If this expertise is not available in your school or school district, reach out to a college or university, health department, or other organization with trained evaluators who may be able to help you. Much of this collaboration can be done electronically, so it is not necessary that your collaborators be located near your school.

To learn more about program evaluation for your comprehensive school physical activity program, see the Centers for Disease Control and Prevention (CDC, 2013) guide "Comprehensive School Physical Activity Programs: A Guide for Schools." Another resource is part three of the book *Physical Activity Interventions in Children and Adolescents* (Ward et al., 2007), which provides detailed information and examples on measurement, process evaluation, and impact and outcome evaluation in physical activity programs for youth.

Summary

A comprehensive school physical activity program has five coordinated components to provide students with a variety of daily physical activity opportunities in a supportive school environment. Comprehensive school physical activity programs have positive effects on physical activity levels, fitness, motor skills, and sedentary behavior. The school physical activity committee, with the leadership and facilitation from the school physical activity coordinator, oversees the comprehensive school physical activity program. To learn from experience, it is useful to monitor attendance at the physical activity opportunities and get the reactions of students, staff, and parents to program activities. Work with collaborators who have evaluation expertise to conduct a more detailed evaluation of your comprehensive school physical activity program.

SOURCES AND RESOURCES

Introduction

Centers for Disease Control and Prevention (CDC). 2018. Strategies for classroom physical activity in schools. www.cdc.gov/healthyschools/physicalactivity/pdf/ClassroomPAStrategies_508.pdf

Hayes, G., Dowd, K.P., MacDonncha, C., & Donnelly, A.E. 2019. Tracking of physical activity and sedentary behavior from adolescence to young adulthood: A systematic literature review. *Journal of Adolescent Health, 65*(4): 446-454.

Howie, E.K., McVeigh, J.A., Smith, A.J., Zabatiero, J., Bucks, R.S., Mori, T.A., Bellin, L.J, & Straker, L.M. 2020. Physical activity trajectories from childhood to late adolescence and their implications for health in young adulthood. *Preventive Medicine, 139*, 106224. https://doi.org/10.1016/j.ypmed.2020.106224

Lopes, L., Santos, R., Coelho-e-Silva, M., Draper, C., Mota, J., Jidovtseff, B., Clark, C., et al. 2021. A narrative review of motor competence in children and adolescents: What we know and what we need to find out. *International Journal of Environmental Research and Public Health, 18*(1): 18. https://doi.org/10.3390/ijerph18010018

McMullen, J. & Walton-Fisette, J. 2022. Equity-minded community involvement and family engagement strategies for health and physical educators. *Journal of Physical Education, Recreation & Dance, 93*(2): 46-50.

Merlo, C.L., Everett Jones, S., Michael, S.L., Chen, T.J, Sliwa, S.A., Lee, S.H., Brener, N.D., et al. 2020. Dietary and physical activity behaviors among high school students—Youth Risk Behavior Survey, United States, 2019. *MMWR Supplements, 69*(1): 64.

Powell, K.E., King, A.C., Buchner, D.M., Campbell, W.W., DiPietro, L., Erickson, K.I., Whitt-Glover, M.C., et al. 2018. The scientific foundation for the physical activity guidelines for Americans. *Journal of Physical Activity and Health, 16*(1), 1-11.

Robinson, L.E., Stodden, D.F., Barnett, L.M., Lopes, V.P., Logan. S.W., Rodrigues, L.P., & D'Hondt, E. 2015. Motor competence and its effect on positive developmental trajectories of health. *Sports Med 45*, 1273-1284. https://doi.org/10.1007/s40279-015-0351-6

U.S. Department of Health and Human Services (HHS). 2018a. 2018 physical activity guidelines advisory committee scientific report. https://health.gov/sites/default/files/2019-09/PAG_Advisory_Committee_Report.pdf

U.S. Department of Health and Human Services (HHS). 2018b. *Physical activity guidelines for Americans* (2nd ed.). https://health.gov/sites/default/files/2019-09/Physical_Activity_Guidelines_2nd_edition.pdf

Chapter 1

Bassett, D.R., Fitzhugh, E.C., Heath, G.W., Erwin, P.C., Frederick, G.M., Wolff, D.L., Welch, W.A., & Stout, A.B. 2013. Estimated energy expenditures for school-based policies and active living. *American Journal of Preventive Medicine, 44*(2): 108-113.

Centers for Disease Control and Prevention (CDC). 2018. Strategies for classroom physical activity in schools. www.cdc.gov/healthyschools/physicalactivity/pdf/ClassroomPAStrategies_508.pdf

Centers for Disease Control and Prevention (CDC). n.d. Springboard to Action. Classroom Physical Activity Ideas and Tips. www.cdc.gov/healthyschools/physicalactivity/pdf/Classroom_PA_Ideas_and_Tips_FINAL_201008.pdf

Community Preventive Services Task Force. 2021. Physical activity: Classroom-based physical activity break interventions. The Community Guide. www.thecommunityguide.org/findings/physical-activity-classroom-based-physical-activity-break-interventions

Daly-Smith, A.J., Zwolinsky, S., McKenna, J., Tomporowski, P.D., Defeyter, M.A., & Manley, A. 2018. Systematic review of acute physically active learning and classroom movement breaks on children's physical activity, cognition, academic performance and classroom behaviour: Understanding critical design features. *BMJ Open Sport & Exercise Medicine, 4*(1): e000341.

Hillman, C.H., Logan, N.E., & Shigeta, T.T. 2019. A review of acute physical activity effects on brain and cognition in children. *Translational Journal of the American College of Sports Medicine, 4*(17): 132-136.

Le Fevre, D.N. 2012. *Best new games* (updated edition). Human Kinetics.

Masini, A., Marini, S., Gori, D., Leoni, E., Rochira, A., & Dallolio, L. 2020. Evaluation of school-based interventions of active breaks in primary schools: A systematic review and meta-analysis. *Journal of Science and Medicine in Sport, 23*(4): 377-384.

Michael, R.D., Webster, C.A., Egan, C.A., Nilges, L., Brian, A., Johnson, R., & Carson, R.S. 2019. Facilitators and barriers to movement integration in elementary classrooms: A systematic review. *Research Quarterly for Exercise and Sport, 90*(2): 151-162.

Moon, J., Webster, C.A., Herring, J., & Egan, C.A. 2020. Relationships between systematically observed movement integration and classroom management in elementary schools. *Journal of Positive Behavior Interventions.* https://doi.org/1098300720947034

North Carolina Healthy Schools. NC Healthy Schools | NC DPI K-5 Classroom Energizers K-5 Energizers 2015.pdf - Google Drive

Salmon, J., Mazzoli, E., Lander, N., Contardo Ayala, A.M., Sherar, L., & Ridgers, N.D. 2020. Classroom-based physical activity interventions. In *The Routledge Handbook of Youth Physical Activity*, pp. 523-540. Routledge.

Sember, V., Jurak, G., Kovač, M., Morrison, S.A., & Starc, G. 2020. Children's physical activity, academic performance, and cognitive functioning: A systematic review and meta-analysis. *Frontiers in Public Health*, 8: 307.

U.S. Department of Health and Human Services (HHS). 2018. 2018 physical activity guidelines advisory committee scientific report. https://health.gov/sites/default/files/2019-09/PAG_Advisory_Committee_Report.pdf

Van den Berg, V., Salimi, R., De Groot, R.H.M., Jolles, J., Chinapaw, M.J.M., & Singh, A.S. 2017. "It's a battle . . . you want to do it, but how will you get it done?": Teachers' and principals' perceptions of implementing additional physical activity in school for academic performance. *International Journal of Environmental Research and Public Health*, 14(10): 1160.

Chapter 2

Centers for Disease Control and Prevention (CDC). 2018. Strategies for Classroom Physical Activity in Schools. www.cdc.gov/healthyschools/physicalactivity/pdf/ClassroomPAStrategies_508.pdf

Centers for Disease Control and Prevention (CDC). n.d. Springboard to Action. Classroom Physical Activity Ideas and Tips. www.cdc.gov/healthyschools/physicalactivity/pdf/Classroom_PA_Ideas_and_Tips_FINAL_201008.pdf

Community Preventive Services Task Force. 2021. Physical activity: Classroom-based physically active lesson interventions. The Community Guide. www.thecommunityguide.org/content/tffrs-physical-activity-classroom-based-physically-active-lesson-interventions

Daly-Smith, A.J., Zwolinsky, S., McKenna, J., Tomporowski, P.D., Defeyter, M.A., & Manley, A. 2018. Systematic review of acute physically active learning and classroom movement breaks on children's physical activity, cognition, academic performance and classroom behaviour: Understanding critical design features. *BMJ Open Sport & Exercise Medicine*, 4(1): e000341.

Hillman, C.H., Logan, N.E., & Shigeta, T.T. 2019. A review of acute physical activity effects on brain and cognition in children. *Translational Journal of the American College of Sports Medicine*, 4(17): 132-136.

Le Fevre, D.N. 2012. *Best new games* (updated edition). Human Kinetics.

Michael, R.D., Webster, C.A., Egan, C.A., Nilges, L., Brian, A., Johnson, R., & Carson, R.S. 2019. Facilitators and barriers to movement integration in elementary classrooms: A systematic review. *Research Quarterly for Exercise and Sport*, 90(2): 151-162.

Moon, J., Webster, C.A., Herring, J., & Egan, C.A. 2020. Relationships between systematically observed movement integration and classroom management in elementary schools. *Journal of Positive Behavior Interventions*. https://doi.org/1098300720947034

Norris, E., van Steen, T., Direito, A., & Stamatakis, E. 2020. Physically active lessons in schools and their impact on physical activity, educational, health and cognition outcomes: A systematic review and meta-analysis. *British Journal of Sports Medicine*, 54(14): 826-838.

North Carolina Department of Public Instruction. NC Healthy Schools. K-5 Classroom Energizers. https://sites.google.com/dpi.nc.gov/nchealthfulliving/physical-activity?authuser=0

Sember, V., Jurak, G., Kovač, M., Morrison, S.A., & Starc, G. 2020. Children's physical activity, academic performance, and cognitive functioning: A systematic review and meta-analysis. *Frontiers in Public Health*, 8: 307.

U.S. Department of Health and Human Services (HHS). 2018. 2018 physical activity guidelines advisory committee scientific report. https://health.gov/sites/default/files/2019-09/PAG_Advisory_Committee_Report.pdf

Van den Berg, V., Salimi, R., De Groot, R.H.M., Jolles, J., Chinapaw, M.J.M., & Singh, A.S. 2017. "It's a battle . . . you want to do it, but how will you get it done?": Teachers' and principals' perceptions of implementing additional physical activity in school for academic performance. *International Journal of Environmental Research and Public Health, 14*(10): 1160.

Chapter 3

Alfredsson, L., Armstrong, B.K., Butterfield, D.A., Chowdhury, R., de Gruijl, F.R., Feelisch, M., Garland, C.F., et al. 2020. Insufficient sun exposure has become a real public health problem. *International Journal of Environmental Research and Public Health, 17*(14): 5014.

Bergeron, M.F. 2015. Hydration in the pediatric athlete—How to guide your patients. *Current Sports Medicine Reports, 14*(4): 288-293.

Brittin, J., Sorensen, D., Trowbridge, M., Lee, K.K., Breithecker, D., Frerichs, L., & Huang, T. 2015. Physical activity design guidelines for school architecture. *PloS ONE, 10*(7): e0132597.

Centers for Disease Control and Prevention (CDC). 2002. Guidelines for school programs to prevent skin cancer. www.cdc.gov/cancer/skin/what_cdc_is_doing/guidelines.htm

Centers for Disease Control and Prevention (CDC). 2014. Increasing access to drinking water in schools. www.cdc.gov/healthyschools/npao/pdf/water_access_in_schools_508.pdf.

Centers for Disease Control and Prevention (CDC) and SHAPE America. 2017a. Strategies for recess in schools. www.cdc.gov/healthyschools/physicalactivity/pdf/2016_12_16_schoolrecessstrategies_508.pdf.

Centers for Disease Control and Prevention (CDC) and SHAPE America. 2017b. Recess planning in schools: A guide to putting strategies for recess into practice. www.cdc.gov/healthyschools/physicalactivity/pdf/2016_12_16_schoolrecessplanning_508.pdf

Council on School Health. 2013. The crucial role of recess in school. *Pediatrics, 131*(1): 183-188.

Erem, A.S. & Razzaque, M.R. 2021. Vitamin D-independent benefits of safe sunlight exposure. *The Journal of Steroid Biochemistry and Molecular Biology, 213*: 105957.

Gardner, H. 2017. *Physical literacy on the move: Games for developing confidence and competence in physical activity.* Human Kinetics.

Gray, C., Gibbons, R., Larouche, R., Sandseter, E.B.H., Bienenstock, A., Brussoni, M., Chabot, G., et al. 2015. What is the relationship between outdoor time and physical activity, sedentary behaviour, and physical fitness in children? A systematic review. *International Journal of Environmental Research and Public Health, 12*(6): 6455-6474.

Heidorn, J. & Heidorn, B. 2018. Recess reboot: Effective planning and implementation strategies for classroom teachers. *Strategies, 31*(5): 48-52.

Hillman, C.H., Logan, N.E., & Shigeta, T.T. 2019. A review of acute physical activity effects on brain and cognition in children. *Translational Journal of the American College of Sports Medicine, 4*(17): 132-136.

Le Fevre, D.N. 2012. *Best new games* (updated edition). Human Kinetics.

Kenney, E.L., Long, M.W., Cradock, A.L., & Gortmaker, S.L. 2015. Prevalence of inadequate hydration among US children and disparities by gender and race/ethnicity: National Health and Nutrition Examination Survey, 2009–2012. *American Journal of Public Health*, 105(8): e113-e118.

Khan, N.A., Westfall, D.R., Jones, A.R., Sinn, M.A., Bottin, J.H., Perrier, E.T., & Hillman, C.H. 2019. A 4-d water intake intervention increases hydration and cognitive flexibility among preadolescent children. *The Journal of Nutrition*, 149(12): 2255-2264.

Massey, W.V., Stellino, M.B., & Fraser, M. 2018. Individual and environmental correlates of school-based recess engagement. *Preventive medicine reports, 11*: 247-253.

Massey, W.V., Perez, D., Neilson, L., Thalken, J., & Szarabajko, A. 2021. Observations from the playground: Common problems and potential solutions for school-based recess. *Health Education Journal, 80*(3): 313-326.

McMullen, J. & Walton-Fisette, J. 2022. Equity-minded community involvement and family engagement strategies for health and physical educators. *Journal of Physical Education, Recreation & Dance, 93*(2): 46-50.

Merhej, R. Dehydration and cognition: An understated relation. 2018. *International Journal of Health Governance*. https://doi.org/10.1108/IJHG-10-2018-0056

Nathan, N., Elton, B., Babic, M., McCarthy, N., Sutherland, R., Presseau, J., Seward, K., et al. 2018. Barriers and facilitators to the implementation of physical activity policies in schools: A systematic review. *Preventive Medicine, 107*: 45-53.

Orlick, T. 2006. *Cooperative games and sports* (2nd ed.). Human Kinetics.

Parrish, A.M., Chong, K.H., Moriarty, A.L., Batterham, M., & Ridgers, N.D. 2020. Interventions to change school recess activity levels in children and adolescents: A systematic review and meta-analysis. *Sports Medicine, 50*(12): 2145-2173.

Pate, R.R., Dowda, M., Dishman, R.K., Colabianchi, N., Saunders, R.P., & McIver, K.L. 2019. Change in children's physical activity: Predictors in the transition from elementary to middle school. *American Journal Preventive Medicine, 56*(3): e65-e73.

U.S. Department of Health and Human Services (HHS). 2018. 2018 physical activity guidelines advisory committee scientific report. https://health.gov/sites/default/files/2019-09/PAG_Advisory_Committee_Report.pdf

Pulido Sánchez, S. & Iglesias Gallego, D. 2021. Evidence-based overview of accelerometer-measured physical activity during school recess: An updated systematic review. *International Journal of Environmental Research and Public Health, 18*(2): 578.

Ridgers, N.D., Salmon, J., Parrish, A-M., Stanley, R.M., & Okely, A.D. 2012. Physical activity during school recess: A systematic review. *American Journal of Preventive Medicine, 43*(3): 320-328.

Ridgers, N.D., Parrish, A-M., Salmon, J., & Timperio, A. 2020. School recess physical activity interventions. In *The Routledge handbook of youth physical activity* (pp. 504-522). Routledge.

Yogman, M., Garner, A., Hutchinson, J., Hirsh-Pasek, K., Michnick Golinkoff, R., Baum, R., Gambon, T., et al. 2018. The power of play: A pediatric role in enhancing development in young children. *Pediatrics, 142*(3): e20182058.

Chapter 4

Baeten, M., Dochy, F., Struyven, K., Parmentier, E., & Vanderbruggen, A. 2016. Student-centered learning environments: An investigation into student teachers' instructional preferences and approaches to learning. *Learning Environments Research, 19*(1): 43-62.

Brittin, J., Sorensen, D., Trowbridge, M., Lee, K.K., Breithecker, D., Frerichs, L., & Huang, T. 2015. Physical activity design guidelines for school architecture. *PloS ONE, 10*(7): e0132597.

Byun, W., Blair, S.N., & Pate, R.R. 2013. Objectively measured sedentary behavior in preschool children: Comparison between Montessori and traditional preschools. *International Journal of Behavioral Nutrition and Physical Activity, 10*(1): 1-7.

Hillman, C.H., Logan, N.E., & Shigeta, T.T. 2019. A review of acute physical activity effects on brain and cognition in children. *Translational Journal of the American College of Sports Medicine, 4*(17): 132-136.

Kaput, K. 2018. Evidence for student-centered learning. Education Evolving. https://files.eric.ed.gov/fulltext/ED581111.pdf

Kariippanon, K.E., Cliff, D.P., Lancaster, S.L., Okely, A.D., & Parrish, A,-M. 2018. Perceived interplay between flexible learning spaces and teaching, learning and student wellbeing. *Learning Environments Research, 21*(3: 301-320.

Kariippanon, K.E., Cliff, D.P., Okely, A.D., & Parrish, A.M. 2020. The "why" and "how" of flexible learning spaces: A complex adaptive systems analysis. *Journal of Educational Change 21*(4): 569-593.

Kariippanon, K.E., Cliff, D.P., Ellis, Y.G., Ucci, M., Okely, A.D., & Parrish, A.-M. 2021. School flexible learning spaces, student movement behavior and educational outcomes among adolescents: A mixed-methods systematic review. *Journal of School Health, 91*(2): 133-145.

Koestner, R., Ryan, R.M., Bernieri, F., & Holt, K. 1984. Setting limits on children's behavior: The differential effects of controlling vs. informational styles on intrinsic motivation and creativity. *Journal of Personality, 52*(3): 233-248.

Lillard, A.S. 2019. Shunned and admired: Montessori, self-determination, and a case for radical school reform. *Educational Psychology Review, 31*(4): 939-965.

Lubans, D.R., Lonsdale, C., Cohen, K., Eather, N., Beauchamp, M.R., Morgan, P.J., Sylvester, B.D., & Smith, J.J. 2017. Framework for the design and delivery of organized physical activity sessions for children and adolescents: Rationale and description of the 'SAAFE' teaching principles. *International Journal of Behavioral Nutrition and Physical Activity, 14*(1): 1-11.

Marshall, C. 2017. Montessori education: A review of the evidence base. *npj Science of Learning, 2*(1): 1-9.

Niemiec, C.P. & Ryan, R.M. 2009. Autonomy, competence, and relatedness in the classroom: Applying self-determination theory to educational practice. *Theory and Research in Education, 7*(2): 133-144.

Norris, E., van Steen, T., Direito, A., & Stamatakis, E. 2020. Physically active lessons in schools and their impact on physical activity, educational, health and cognition outcomes: A systematic review and meta-analysis. *British Journal of Sports Medicine, 54*(14): 826-838.

Pate, R.R., O'Neill, J.R., Byun, W., McIver, K.L., Dowda, M., & Brown, W.H. 2014. Physical activity in preschool children: Comparison between Montessori and traditional preschools. *Journal of School Health, 84*(11): 716-721. https://doi.org/10.1111/josh.12207

Ryan, R.M. & Deci, E.L. 2000. Self-determination theory and the facilitation of intrinsic motivation, social development, and well-being. *American Psychologist, 55*(1): 68.

Chapter 5

Barnett, L.M., Stodden, D., Cohen, K.E., Smith, J.J., Revalds Lubans, D., Lenoir, M., Iivonen, S., et al. 2016. Fundamental movement skills: An important focus. *Journal of Teaching in Physical Education, 35*(3): 219-225.

Community Preventive Services Task Force. 2013. Behavioral and social approaches to increase physical activity: Enhanced school-based physical education. The Community Guide. https://www.thecommunityguide.org/sites/default/files/PA-Behavioral-School-based-PE-Archive.pdf

de Bruijn, A.G.M, Mombarg, R., & Timmermans, A.C. 2022. The importance of satisfying children's basic psychological needs in primary school physical education for PE-motivation, and its relations with fundamental motor and PE-related skills. *Physical Education and Sport Pedagogy, 27*(4): 422-439.

García-Hermoso, A., Alonso-Martínez, A.M., Ramírez-Vélez, R., Pérez-Sousa, M.Á., Ramírez-Campillo, R., & Izquierdo, M. 2020. Association of physical education with improvement of health-related physical fitness outcomes and fundamental motor skills among youths: A systematic review and meta-analysis. *JAMA Pediatrics, 174*(6): e200223-e200223.

Gardner, H. 2017. *Physical literacy on the move: Games for developing confidence and competence in physical activity.* Human Kinetics.

Gleddie, D.L. & Morgan, A. 2021. Physical literacy praxis: A theoretical framework for transformative physical education. *Prospects, 50*(1): 31-53.

Hillman, C.H., Logan, N.E., & Shigeta, T.T. 2019. A review of acute physical activity effects on brain and cognition in children. *Translational Journal of the American College of Sports Medicine, 4*(17): 132-136.

Hollis, J.L., Williams, A.J., Sutherland, R., Campbell, E., Nathan, N., Wolfenden, L., Morgan, P.J., Lubans, D.R., & Wiggers, J. 2016. A systematic review and meta-analysis of moderate-to-vigorous physical activity levels in elementary school physical education lessons. *Preventive medicine*, 86: 34-54.

Le Fevre, D.N. 2012. *Best new games* (updated edition). Human Kinetics.

Lonsdale, C., Rosenkranz, R.R., Peralta, L.R., Bennie, A., Fahey, P., & Lubans, D.R. 2013. A systematic review and meta-analysis of interventions designed to increase moderate-to-vigorous physical activity in school physical education lessons. *Preventive Medicine, 56*(2): 152-61.

Lorås, H. 2020. The effects of physical education on motor competence in children and adolescents: a systematic review and meta-analysis. *Sports 8*(6): 88.

Lubans, D.R., Lonsdale, C., Cohen, K., Eather, N., Beauchamp, M.R., Morgan, P.J., Sylvester, B.D., & Smith, J.J. 2017. Framework for the design and delivery of organized physical activity sessions for children and adolescents: Rationale and description of the SAAFE teaching principles. *International Journal of Behavioral Nutrition and Physical Activity, 14*(1): 1-11.

Luepker, R.V., Perry, C.L., McKinlay, S.M., Nader, P.R., Parcel, G.S., Stone, E.J., Webber, L.S., et al. 1996. Outcomes of a field trial to improve children's dietary patterns and physical Activity. The Child and Adolescent Trial for Cardiovascular Health (CATCH). *JAMA*, 275(10): 768-776.

McKenzie, T.L., Sallis, J.F., Rosengard, P., & Ballard, K. 2016. The SPARK programs: A public health model of physical education research and dissemination. *Journal of Teaching in Physical Education*, 35(4): 381-389.

Niemiec, C.P. & Ryan, R.M. 2009. Autonomy, competence, and relatedness in the classroom: Applying self-determination theory to educational practice. *Theory and Research in Education*, 7(2): 133-144.

Powell, E., Woodfield, L.A., & Nevill, A.M. 2016. Increasing physical activity levels in primary school physical education: The SHARP Principles model. *Preventive Medicine Reports*, 3: 7-13.

Robinson, L.E., Stodden, D.F., Barnett, L.M., Lopes, V.P., Logan, S.W., Rodrigues, L.P., & D'Hondt, E. 2015. Motor competence and its effect on positive developmental trajectories of health. *Sports Medicine*, 45(9): 1273-1284.

Ryan, R.M. & Deci, E.L. 2000. Self-determination theory and the facilitation of intrinsic motivation, social development, and well-being. *American Psychologist*, 55(1): 68.

Sallis, J.F., McKenzie, T.L., Alcaraz, J.E., Kolody, B., Faucette, N., & Hovell, M.F. 1997. The effects of a 2-year physical education program (SPARK) on physical activity and fitness in elementary school students. Sports, Play and Active Recreation for Kids. *American Journal of Public Health*, 87(8): 1328-1334.

Sun, H., Li, W., & Shen, B. 2017. Learning in physical education: A self-determination theory perspective. *Journal of Teaching in Physical Education*, 36 (3): 277-291.

Tompsett, C., Sanders, R., Taylor, C., & Cobley, S. 2017. Pedagogical approaches to and effects of fundamental movement skill interventions on health outcomes: A systematic review. *Sports Medicine* 47(9): 1795-1819.

U.S. Department of Health and Human Services (HHS). 2018. 2018 physical activity guidelines advisory committee scientific report. https://health.gov/sites/default/files/2019-09/PAG_Advisory_Committee_Report.pdf

Vasconcellos, D., Parker, P.D., Hilland, T., Cinelli, R., Owen, K.B., Kapsal, N., Lee, J., et al. 2020. Self-determination theory applied to physical education: A systematic review and meta-analysis. *Journal of Educational Psychology*, 112(7): 1444.

Weaver, R.G, Webster, C., & Beets, M.W. 2013. Let us play: Maximizing physical activity in physical education. *Strategies*, 26(6): 33-37.

Wong, L.S., Gibson, A.-M., Farooq, A., & Reilly, J.J. 2021. Interventions to increase moderate-to-vigorous physical activity in elementary school physical education lessons: Systematic review. *Journal of School Health*, 91(10): 836-845.

Chapter 6

Adams, V. 2019. Steps to increase family and community engagement in elementary school. *Strategies*, 32(4): 29-32.

Beni, S., Fletcher, T., & Chróinín, D.N. 2017. Meaningful experiences in physical education and youth sport: A review of the literature. *Quest*, 69(3): 291-312.

Cale, L. & Harris, J. 2018. The role of knowledge and understanding in fostering physical literacy. *Journal of Teaching in Physical Education*, 37(3): 280-287.

Centers for Disease Control and Prevention (CDC). 2013. Comprehensive school physical activity programs: A guide for schools. www.cdc.gov/healthyschools/physicalactivity/pdf/13_242620-A_CSPAP_SchoolPhysActivityPrograms_Final_508_12192013.pdf

Community Preventive Services Task Force. 2014. Behavioral and social approaches to increase physical activity: Enhanced school-based physical education. www.thecommunityguide.org/sites/default/files/assets/PA-Behavioral-School-based-PE.pdf

Dowda, M., Saunders, R.P., Colabianchi, N., Dishman, R.K., McIver, K.L., & Pate, R.R. 2020. Longitudinal associations between psychosocial, home, and neighborhood factors and children's physical activity. *Journal of Physical Activity and Health, 17*(3): 306-312.

Egan, C.A. & Miller, M. 2019. Family and community involvement to increase physical activity as part of a CSPAP. *Journal of Physical Education, Recreation & Dance, 90*(1): 39-45.

Ennis, C.D. 2017. Educating students for a lifetime of physical activity: Enhancing mindfulness, motivation, and meaning. *Research Quarterly for Exercise and Sport, 88*(3): 241-250.

García–Hermoso, A., Alonso-Martínez, A.M., Ramírez-Vélez, R., Pérez-Sousa, M.A., Ramírez-Campillo, R., & Izquierdo, M. 2020. Association of physical education with improvement of health-related physical fitness outcomes and fundamental motor skills among youths: A systematic review and meta-analysis. *JAMA Pediatrics, 174*(6): e200223-e200223.

Gerards, S.M.P.L., Van Kann, D.H.H., Kremers, S.P.J., Jansen, M.W.J., & Gubbels, J.S. 2021. Do parenting practices moderate the association between the physical neighbourhood environment and changes in children's time spent at various physical activity levels? An exploratory longitudinal study. *BMC Public Health, 21*(1): 1-12.

Harrington, D.M., Gillison, F., Broyles, S.T., Chaput, J.-P., Fogelholm, M., Hu, G., Kuriyan, R., et al. 2016. Household-level correlates of children's physical activity levels in and across 12 countries. *Obesity, 24*(10): 2150-2157.

Hollis, J.L., Williams, A.J., Sutherland, R., Campbell, E., Nathan, N., Wolfenden, L., Morgan, P.J., Lubans, D.R., & Wiggers, J. 2016. A systematic review and meta-analysis of moderate-to-vigorous physical activity levels in elementary school physical education lessons. *Preventive Medicine, 86*: 34-54.

Jaeschke, L., Steinbrecher, A., Luzak, A., Puggina, A., Aleksovska, K., Buck, C., Burns, C., et al. 2017. Socio-cultural determinants of physical activity across the life course: A "Determinants of Diet and Physical Activity" (DEDIPAC) umbrella systematic literature review. *International Journal of Behavioral Nutrition and Physical Activity, 14*(1): 1-15.

Ladwig, M.A., Vazou, S., & Ekkekakis, P. 2018. "My best memory is when I was done with it": PE memories are associated with adult sedentary behavior. *Translational Journal of the American College of Sports Medicine, 3*(16): 119-129.

Lonsdale, C., Rosenkranz, R.R., Peralta, L.R., Bennie, A., Fahey, P., & Lubans, D.R. 2013. A systematic review and meta-analysis of interventions designed to increase moderate-to-vigorous physical activity in school physical education lessons. *Preventive Medicine, 56*(2):152-61.

Lubans, D.R., Lonsdale, C., Cohen, K., Eather, N., Beauchamp, M.R., Morgan, P.J., Sylvester, B.D., & Smith, J.J. 2017. Framework for the design and delivery of organized physical activity sessions for children and adolescents: Rationale and description of the 'SAAFE' teaching principles. *International Journal of Behavioral Nutrition and Physical Activity, 14*(1): 1-11.

McMullen, J. & Walton-Fisette, J. 2022. Equity-minded community involvement and family engagement strategies for health and physical educators. *Journal of Physical Education, Recreation & Dance, 93*(2): 46-50.

Ní Chróinín, D., Fletcher, T., & O'Sullivan, M. 2018. Pedagogical principles of learning to teach meaningful physical education. *Physical Education and Sport Pedagogy, 23*(2): 117-133.

Niemiec, C.P. & Ryan, R.M. 2009. Autonomy, competence, and relatedness in the classroom: Applying self-determination theory to educational practice. *Theory and Research in Education, 7*(2): 133-144.

Pate, R.R., Dowda, M., Dishman, R.K., Colabianchi, N., Saunders, R.P., & McIver, K.L. 2019. Change in children's physical activity: Predictors in the transition from elementary to middle school. *American Journal of Preventive Medicine, 56*(3): e65-e73.

Pate, R.R., Davis, M.G., Robinson, T.N., Stone, E.J., McKenzie, T.L., & Young, J.C. 2006. Promoting physical activity in children and youth: A leadership role for schools: A scientific statement from the American Heart Association Council on Nutrition, Physical Activity, and Metabolism (Physical Activity Committee) in collaboration with the Councils on Cardiovascular Disease in the Young and Cardiovascular Nursing. *Circulation, 114*(11): 1214-1224.

Pereira, P., Marinho, D.A., & Santos, F. 2021. Positive motivational climates, physical activity and sport participation through self-determination theory: Striving for quality physical education. *Journal of Physical Education, Recreation & Dance, 92*(6): 42-47.

Ryan, R.M. & Deci, E.L. 2000. Self-determination theory and the facilitation of intrinsic motivation, social development, and well-being. *American Psychologist, 55*(1): 68.

Sun, H., Li, W., & Shen, Bo. 2017. Learning in physical education: A self-determination theory perspective. *Journal of Teaching in Physical Education, 36*(3): 277-291.

U.S. Department of Health and Human Services (HHS). 2018a. 2018 physical activity guidelines advisory committee scientific report. https://health.gov/sites/default/files/2019-09/PAG_Advisory_Committee_Report.pdf

U.S. Department of Health and Human Services (HHS). 2018b. *Physical activity guidelines for Americans* (2nd ed.). https://health.gov/sites/default/files/2019-09/Physical_Activity_Guidelines_2nd_edition.pdf

Vasconcellos, D., Parker, P.D., Hilland, T., Cinelli, R., Owen, K.B., Kapsal, N., Lee, J., et al. 2020. Self-determination theory applied to physical education: A systematic review and meta-analysis. *Journal of Educational Psychology, 112*(7): 1444.

Webster, C.A., Rink, J.E., Carson, R.L., Moon, J., & Gaudreault, K.L. 2020. The comprehensive school physical activity program model: A proposed illustrative supplement to help move the needle on youth physical activity. *Kinesiology Review 9*(2): 112-121.

Wilkie, H.J., Standage, M., Gillison, F.B., Cumming, S.B., & Katzmarzyk, P.T. 2018. Correlates of intensity-specific physical activity in children aged 9–11 years: A multilevel analysis of UK data from the International Study of Childhood Obesity, Lifestyle and the Environment. *BMJ Open, 8*(2): e018373.

Wong, L.S., Gibson, A.-M., Farooq, A., & Reilly, J.J. 2021. Interventions to increase moderate-to-vigorous physical activity in elementary school physical education lessons: Systematic review. *Journal of School Health, 91*(10): 836-845.

Chapter 7

Belton, S. & O'Brien, W. 2020. Before- and after-school interventions in youth physical activity: Current situation and future directions. In T.A. Brusseau, S.J. Fairclough, & D.R. Lubans (Eds.), *The Routledge handbook of youth physical activity* (pp. 636-648). Routledge.

Build Our Kids' Success (BOKS). n.d. www.bokskids.org

Buttazzoni, A.N., Coen, S.E., & Gilliland, J.A. 2018. Supporting active school travel: A qualitative analysis of implementing a regional safe routes to school program. *Social Science & Medicine, 212*: 181-190.

Centers for Disease Control and Prevention (CDC). 2013. Comprehensive school physical activity programs: A guide for schools. www.cdc.gov/healthyschools/physicalactivity/pdf/13_242620-A_CSPAP_SchoolPhysActivityPrograms_Final_508_12192013.pdf

Community Preventive Services Task Force. 2018. Physical activity: Interventions to increase active travel to school. www.thecommunityguide.org/content/interventions-increase-active-travel-school

Cradock, A.L., Barrett, J.L., Taveras, E.M., Peabody, S., Flax, C.N., Giles, C.M., & Gortmaker, S.L. 2019. Effects of a before-school program on student physical activity levels. *Preventive Medicine Reports, 15*: 100940.

Demetriou, Y., Gillison, F., & McKenzie, T.L. 2017. After-school physical activity interventions on child and adolescent physical activity and health: A review of reviews. *Advances in Physical Education, 7*(2): 191-215.

Ikeda, E., Mandic, S., Smith, M., Stewart, T., & Duncan, S. 2020. Active transport. In T.A. Brusseau, S.J. Fairclough, & D.R. Lubans (Eds.), *The Routledge handbook of youth physical activity* (pp. 665-685). Routledge.

Jones, R.A., Blackburn, N.E., Woods, C., Byrne, M., van Nassau, F., & Tully, M.A. 2019. Interventions promoting active transport to school in children: A systematic review and meta-analysis. *Preventive Medicine, 123*: 232-241.

Kontou, E., McDonald, N.C., Brookshire, K., Pullen-Seufert, N.C., & LaJeunesse, S. 2020. US active school travel in 2017: Prevalence and correlates. *Preventive Medicine Reports, 17*: 101024.

Larouche, R., Mammen, G., Rowe, D.A., & Faulkner, G. 2018. Effectiveness of active school transport interventions: A systematic review and update. *BMC Public Health, 18*(1): 1-18.

McDonald, N.C., Steiner, R.L., Lee, C., Rhoulac Smith, T., Zhu, X., & Yang, Y. 2014. Impact of the Safe Routes to School program on walking and bicycling. *Journal of the American Planning Association, 80*(2): 153-167.

National Center for Safe Routes to School. n.d. Starting a walking school bus. http://walkingschoolbus.org/

Omura, J.D., Hyde, E.T., Watson, K.B., Sliwa, S.A., Fulton, J.E., & Carlson, S.A. 2019. Prevalence of children walking to school and related barriers—United States, 2017. *Preventive Medicine, 118*: 191-195.

Price-Shingles, J.N. & Place, G. 2016. Seven steps for implementing afterschool programs: Strategies for physical educators. *Strategies, 29*(2): 34-38.

Safe Routes. n.d. The walking school bus: Combining safety, fun, and the walk to school. http://guide.saferoutesinfo.org/pdf/wsb_guide.pdf

Safe Routes to School. n.d.a. Introduction to safe routes to school: The healthy, safety, and transportation nexus. guide.saferoutesinfo.org/introduction/index.cfm

Safe Routes to School. n.d.b. Steps to creating a safe routes to school program. http://guide.saferoutesinfo.org/steps/?msclkid=079dbe60b50a11ec971b64e-d51ac9d59

Smith, L., Norgate, S.H., Cherrett, T., Davies, N., Winstanley, C., & Harding, M. 2015. Walking school buses as a form of active transportation for children—A review of the evidence. *Journal of School Health, 85*(3): 197-210.

Woodforde, J., Alsop, T., Salmon, J., Gomersall, J., & Stylianou, M. 2021. Effects of school-based before-school physical activity programmes on children's physical activity levels, health and learning-related outcomes: A systematic review. *British Journal of Sports Medicine, 56*(13): 740-754.

Chapter 8

Acosta, M.E., Matsuzaki, M., Slater, S.J., & Sanchez-Vaznaugh, E.V. 2021. Physical activity strategies in low-resource elementary schools: Why and how are they prioritized? *Preventive Medicine Reports, 23*: 101430.

An, R., Liu, J., & Liu, R. 2021. State laws governing school physical education in relation to attendance and physical activity among students in the USA: A systematic review and meta-analysis. *Journal of Sport and Health Science, 10*(3): 277-287.

Brittin, J., Sorensen, D., Trowbridge, M., Lee, K.K., Breithecker, D., Frerichs, L., & Huang, T. 2015. Physical activity design guidelines for school architecture. *PloS ONE, 10*(7): e0132597.

Centers for Disease Control and Prevention (CDC). n.d. School connectedness. www.cdc.gov/healthyyouth/protective/school_connectedness.htm

Centers for Disease Control and Prevention (CDC). 2013. Comprehensive school physical activity programs: A guide for schools. www.cdc.gov/healthyschools/physicalactivity/pdf/13_242620-A_CSPAP_SchoolPhysActivityPrograms_Final_508_12192013.pdf

Centers for Disease Control and Prevention (CDC). 2016. School health policies and practices study (2016): Physical education and physical activity district questionnaire. www.cdc.gov/healthyyouth/data/shpps/files/questionnaires/2016/SHPPS_Physical_Education_District.pdf

Centers for Disease Control and Prevention (CDC). 2017. School health index: A self-assessment and planning guide (Elementary school version). CDC. www.cdc.gov/healthyschools/shi/pdf/Elementary-Total-2017.pdf

Fair, K.N., Solari Williams, K.D., Warren, J., McKyer, E.L.J., & Ory, M.G. 2018. The influence of organizational culture on school-based obesity prevention interventions: A systematic review of the literature. *Journal of School Health, 88*(6): 462-473.

Gelius, P., Messing, S., Goodwin, L., Schow, D., & Abu-Omar, K. 2020. What are effective policies for promoting physical activity? A systematic review of reviews. *Preventive Medicine Reports, 18*: 101095.

Gray C., Gibbons, R., Larouche, R., Sandseter, E.B.H., Bienenstock, A., Brussoni, M., Chabot, G., et al. 2015. What is the relationship between outdoor time and physical activity, sedentary behaviour, and physical fitness in children? A systematic review. *International Journal of Environmental Research and Public Health, 12*(6): 6455-6474.

Langley, K. & Hodges Kulinna, P. 2018. Developing a staff physical activity program at your school: Implementing the lesser-used component of the CSPAP model. *Journal of Physical Education, Recreation & Dance, 89*(2): 49-55.

London, R.A., Westrich, L., Stokes-Guinan, K., & McLaughlin, M. 2015. Playing fair: The contribution of high-functioning recess to overall school climate in low-income elementary schools. *Journal of School Health, 85*(1): 53-60.

Lounsbery, M.A.F., McKenzie, T.L., Morrow, J.R., Holt, K.A., & Budnar, R.G. 2013. School physical activity policy assessment. *Journal of Physical Activity and Health, 10*(4): 496-503.

Lounsbery, M.A.F. 2017. School physical activity: Policy matters. *Kinesiology Review, 6*(1): 51-59.

Lounsbery, M.A.F., McKenzie, T.L., & Smith, N.J. 2019. School physical activity policy. *Translational Journal of the American College of Sports Medicine, 4*(17): 173-178.

Martin, K., Bremner, A., Salmon, J., Rosenberg, M., & Giles-Corti, B. 2014. Physical, policy, and sociocultural characteristics of the primary school environment are positively associated with children's physical activity during class time. *Journal of Physical Activity and Health, 11*(3): 553-563.

McMullen, J. & Walton-Fisette, J. 2022. Equity-minded community involvement and family engagement strategies for health and physical educators. *Journal of Physical Education, Recreation & Dance, 93*(2): 46-50.

Morton, K.L., Atkin, A.J., Corder, K., Suhrcke, M., & Van Sluijs, E.M.F. 2016. The school environment and adolescent physical activity and sedentary behaviour: A mixed-studies systematic review. *Obesity Reviews, 17*(2): 142-158.

National Association of Chronic Disease Directors (NACDD). 2018. Healthy School, Healthy Staff, Healthy Students. A Guide to Improving School Employee Wellness. https://www.chronicdisease.org/resource/resmgr/school_health/school_employee_wellness/nacdd_schoolemployeewellness.pdf

National Association of State Boards of Education (NASBE). n.d. Health Policies by Category. NASBE State policy database. https://statepolicies.nasbe.org/health/categories

National Physical Activity Alliance. National Physical Activity Plan. n.d. https://paamovewithus.org/for-transfer/education/

Pate, R.R., Dowda, M., Dishman, R.K., Colabianchi, N., Saunders, R.P., & McIver, K.L. 2019. Change in children's physical activity: Predictors in the transition from elementary to middle school. *American Journal of Preventive Medicine, 56*(3): e65-e73.

Walker, T.J., Craig, D.W., Robertson, M.C., Szeszulski, J., & Fernandez, M.E. 2021. The relation between individual-level factors and the implementation of classroom-based physical activity approaches among elementary school teachers. *Translational Behavioral Medicine, 11*(3): 745-753.

Woods, C.B., Volf, K., Kelly, L., Casey, B., Gelius, P., Messing, S., Forberger, S., Lakerveld, J., Zukowska, J., & García Bengoechea, E. 2021. The evidence for the impact of policy on physical activity outcomes within the school setting: A systematic review. *Journal of sport and health science, 10*(3): 263-276.

Wray, A., Martin, G., Ostermeier, E., Medeiros, A., Little, M., Reilly, K., & Gilliland, J. 2020. Evidence synthesis-Physical activity and social connectedness interventions in outdoor spaces among children and youth: A rapid review. *Health Promotion and Chronic Disease Prevention in Canada: Research, Policy and Practice, 40*(4): 104.

Chapter 9

Brusseau, T.A. & Burns, R.D. 2020. Introduction to multicomponent school-based physical activity programs. In T.A. Brusseau, S.J. Fairclough, & D.R. Lubans (Eds.), *The Routledge Handbook of Youth Physical Activity* (pp. 557-576). Routledge.

Carson, R.L., Kuhn, A.P., Moore, J.B., Castelli, D.M., Beighle, A., Hodgin, K.L., & Dauenhauer, B. 2020. Implementation evaluation of a professional development program for comprehensive school physical activity leaders. *Preventive Medicine Reports, 19*: 101109.

Centers for Disease Control and Prevention (CDC). 2013. Comprehensive school physical activity programs: A guide for schools. www.cdc.gov/healthyschools/physicalactivity/pdf/13_242620-A_CSPAP_SchoolPhysActivityPrograms_Final_508_12192013.pdf

Centers for Disease Control and Prevention (CDC). 2019. Increasing physical education and physical activity: A framework for schools. Atlanta, GA: Centers for Disease Control and Prevention, US Dept of Health and Human Services. https://www.cdc.gov/healthyschools/physicalactivity/pdf/2019_04_25_PE-PA-Framework_508tagged.pdf

Centers for Disease Control and Prevention (CDC). 2017. School health index: A self-assessment and planning guide (Elementary school version). CDC. www.cdc.gov/healthyschools/shi/pdf/Elementary-Total-2017.pdf

Chen, S. & Gu, X. 2018. Toward active living: Comprehensive school physical activity program research and implications. *Quest, 70*(2): 191-212.

Erwin, H., Beighle, A., Carson, R.L., & Castelli, D.M. 2013. Comprehensive school-based physical activity promotion: A review. *Quest, 65*(4): 412-428.

Hivner, E., Hoke, A., Francis, E., Ricci, T., Zurlo, C., & Kraschnewski, J. 2019. When a "one size" model doesn't fit all: The Building Healthy Schools program. *Journal of Physical Education, Recreation & Dance, 90*(2): 8-16.

McMullen, J. & Walton-Fisette, J. 2022. Equity-minded community involvement and family engagement strategies for health and physical educators. *Journal of Physical Education, Recreation & Dance, 93*(2): 46-50.

Messing, S., Rütten, A., Abu-Omar, K., Ungerer-Röhrich, U., Goodwin, L., Burlacu, I., & Gediga, G. 2019. How can physical activity be promoted among children and adolescents? A systematic review of reviews across settings. *Frontiers in Public Health, 7*: 55.

Pate, R.R., Davis, M.G., Robinson, T.N., Stone, E.J., McKenzie, T.L., & Young, J.C. 2006. Promoting physical activity in children and youth: A leadership role for schools: A scientific statement from the American Heart Association Council on Nutrition, Physical Activity, and Metabolism (Physical Activity Committee) in collaboration with the Councils on Cardiovascular Disease in the Young and Cardiovascular Nursing. *Circulation, 114*(11): 1214-1224.

Pulling Kuhn, A., Stoepker, P., Dauenhauer, B., & Carson, R.L. 2021. A systematic review of multi-component comprehensive school physical activity program (CSPAP) interventions. *American Journal of Health Promotion, 35*(8): 1129-1149.

U.S. Department of Health and Human Services (HHS). 2018. *Physical activity guidelines for Americans* (2nd ed). https://health.gov/sites/default/files/2019-09/Physical_Activity_Guidelines_2nd_edition.pdf

Ward, D.S., Saunders, R.P., & Pate, R.R. 2007. *Physical activity interventions in children and adolescents.* Human Kinetics.

Webster, C.A., Beets, M., Weaver, R.G., Vazou, S., & Russ, L. 2015. Rethinking recommendations for implementing comprehensive school physical activity programs: A partnership model. *Quest, 67*(2): 185-202.

Webster, C.A., Rink, J.E., Carson, R.L., Moon, J., & Gaudreault, K.L. 2020. The comprehensive school physical activity program model: A proposed illustrative supplement to help move the needle on youth physical activity. *Kinesiology Review, 9*(2): 112-121.

ABOUT THE AUTHORS

Russell R. Pate serves as a professor in the department of exercise science at the University of South Carolina, where his research is focused on physical activity and its promotion among children and adolescents. Also, he has worked extensively on initiatives aimed at advancing the role of physical activity in public health. Pate is a lifelong distance runner, and he has directed two U.S. Olympic marathon trials.

Pate has served as president of the American College of Sports Medicine (ACSM), the National Coalition for Promoting Physical Activity, and the National Physical Activity Plan Alliance. He served on the U.S. Physical Activity Guidelines Advisory Committee in 2008 and 2018. Pate has been recognized by ACSM as its Honor Award recipient, and he received a Lifetime Achievement Award from the President's Council on Physical Fitness and Sports.

Pate received a PhD in exercise physiology from the University of Oregon in 1974. In his free time, he enjoys running, reading, theater, traveling, college sports, and spending time with his family.

Ruth P. Saunders, a professor emerita in the department of health promotion, education, and behavior at the University of South Carolina, has taught and conducted research for over 30 years. She actively participates as a member of the children's physical activity research group in the department of exercise

science and as a co-investigator in the Prevention Research Centers, a program funded by the Centers for Disease Control and Prevention.

Saunders has conducted federally funded and foundation-funded research in schools, preschool centers, children's residential homes, and churches. Her research interests, focused largely on physical activity in children, include organizational-level physical activity interventions, influences on physical activity, and monitoring and evaluating physical activity interventions in organizational settings.

Saunders received her PhD in public health education from the University of South Carolina in 1986. She has received numerous teaching, research, and community volunteer service awards. In her spare time, she enjoys swimming, yoga, writing, and painting.

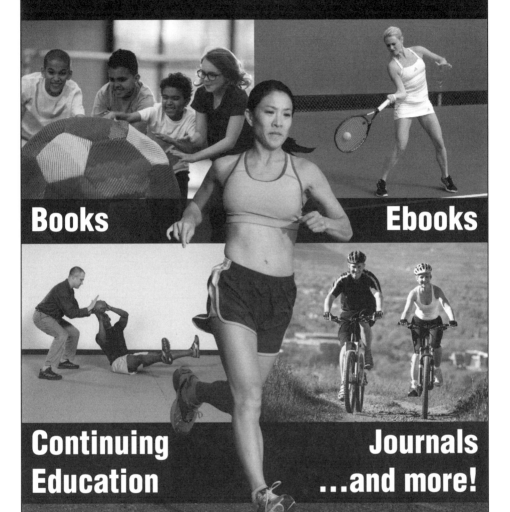